Journey
Into
<u>Usefulness</u>

Journey Into Usefulness

James Mahoney

BROADMAN PRESS
Nashville, Tennessee

Scripture quotations marked TLB are from *The Living Bible, Paraphrased* (Wheaton: Tyndale House Publishers, 1971) and are used by permission.

Scripture quotations marked Phillips are from *The New Testament in Modern English,* © J. B. Phillips, 1958. Used with permission of The Macmillan Company.

Scripture quotations marked Weymouth are from *The New Testament in Modern Speech,* R. F. Weymouth (New York: Harper & Row).

Dewey Decimal Classification: 248.4
Subject heading: CHRISTIAN LIFE//GOD—WILL
Library of Congress Catalog Card Number: 76-9696
Printed in the United States of America

Foreword

If you liked *Journey into Fullness* you will love *Journey into Usefulness*. James Mahoney has produced another masterpiece as practical as it is pointed.

The reader will be informed by its scholarly approach, amused by its "gut-level" honesty, sometimes threatened by its forthright openness, and inspired by its invitation and clarification to the high calling of every believer in Christ Jesus.

Some books are a reading experience and can be picked up, read, and laid down. This volume will not allow that. It demands attention beyond the mere reading. It will not allow you to shrug your shoulders and pass on. You will find that a casual "amen" is not enough. It will take you more time to read this book than most others. You will find yourself looking back in previous chapters, stopping to evaluate your own traditions in the light of new knowledge, and moving with joy into some of the suggestions in the guide sheets.

Dr. Mahoney's treatment of the gifts of the Spirit is one of the most sensible and balanced I have ever read. His coverage of the often misused fleece of Gideon is the most practical presentation I have seen on the subject.

You will discover the illustrations challenging, the projects rewarding, and the exercises priceless. I predict for you, reader, a memorable experience and permanent blessings.

The life of fullness is not merely an experience, though it is that; it is a relationship, not merely a destination but a way of going. This book is a mandate to continue in fullness and through fullness to usefulness.

Thank you, James Mahoney, for another signal contribution in an area of great need. Your writing style, the manner in which your heart comes through your pen makes the ancient observation a pleasant prospect, "Of the making of books there is no end. . . ." Give us more!

JACK R. TAYLOR, *President*
Dimensions in Christian Living

San Antonio, Texas

Introduction

I was not long into my Christian journey before I first began to notice one basic question that all of us have asked over and over again. Like the one melodious strain that recurs throughout a symphony, and like a tune you cannot get off your mind . . . such is the repetition of the question: *"Just how can I know God's will for my life?"*

I have written this book out of empathy and concern for the multiplied thousands of Christians who are less than exuberant about their Christian experience because they have failed to find a satisfactory answer to that question. Uncertain of God's will for their lives, they are "adrift" and usually unproductive.

Some Christians seem to suffer *spiritual anemia.* They lack the strength to do God's will. I wrote my first book with them in mind. It was a book of instruction about spiritual growth and vitality, entitled *Journey into Fullness.*

But countless *other* Christians remain relatively idle in terms of Christian service because they simply have not found God's will for their lives. They feel inept, ill-equipped, and incapable. *It is not that they are resting upon their oars so much as it is a case of learning how and where to row!* This book is written with this second group in mind. Here is the sequel to my first book. Here is a *Journey into USEfulness.*

This book is an attempt to provide a spiritual *apprenticeship* for those who wish to find and follow God's will. It majors on getting you *started.* Therefore, the book attempts to take the broad problem of general guidance and focus it down to a basic path for beginning. That is, the first half of the book narrows to a focus on Christian service as the initial stage of your journey. Then, the book broadens out to supply the necessary principles for plotting the rest of your course into God's perfect will for your life.

Allow me to express a *special* debt of gratitude to *Mrs. Bonnie Kirkley*, who exercised a gift of "ministry" in typing the book in manuscript form. I also wish to thank Mrs. Sharon Hodges for additional mechanical assistance.

HOW TO USE THIS BOOK

As I wrote this book, I had a conference setting in mind. Therefore, the material in some chapters is more of a *study* than a *sermon*. However, I sought to maintain some homiletical form and outline like the arrangement of a sermon.

The setting I have in mind is a *conference*—not a *class*—so I have done more than instruct . . . often resorting to earnest personal entreaty. For instance, I have used the pronoun "you" throughout in order to stay on the plane of the personal and to communicate individually as I would attempt to do in an informal conference setting. And throughout I have sought to detail just what you should do for a proper response.

If you use this book in a small group setting or in a *retreat*, you will notice a page to aid you at the conclusion of each chapter. The format of this book is designed for group study. It provides one chapter a week for *thirteen* weeks. Each chapter concludes with a group exercise for that week. Thirteen weeks is a quarter of study in the church year. A similar study could be made on a church retreat, in a small-group, or home Bible-study group.

If you use this book for sermonic material, I believe the outlines will be rather obvious, and I have attempted to include illustrative material. I would also draw your attention to the footnotes I have included, in order that you might know where to look for additional material.

If you use this book for personal benefit, please realize I have written with *you* in mind . . . so read with the intention of responding!

Contents

I dedicate this book with equal affection to our three daughters.

To *Kaywin:* Intelligent, attractive, and transparently pure . . . a startling contrast to our jaded world.

To *Kim:* Keen of mind, fun-loving, and affectionate . . . a life aglow, who will always be a beautiful delight to those around her.

To *Kelly:* A talented, gorgeous personality who, because of the constant grooming of her mother and older sisters, could some day sing her way into the hearts of the world . . . with a message of Jesus.

But to all three for sharing Christ, singing in our crusades, making those straight A's, and loving Mom and Dad!

1

The Church of Tomorrow

Years ago there was a special exhibit in a world's fair. The exhibit was billed as "The City of Tomorrow." It consisted of a model city, miniature in size but rich in detail and design. The city represented the visual concept of several sociologists and architects concerning what the city of tomorrow would look like. It had double-decker streets. It had moving sidewalks and multi-shaped buildings made of glass. It was beautifully designed, imaginative in architectural expression.

About midway through the fair, a man stood before the model city for a long while. He studied it intently. After a time of concentrated observation, he began to notice something startling. The city had no *churches*. The observer began to inquire and was finally referred to one of the sociologists responsible for the display.

"Why are there no church buildings in this exhibit?" he asked.

"Because," came the reply, *"our studies indicate there will be no churches in the city of tomorrow!"*

Don't you believe it!

The church has often appeared on the casualty list of one "prophet of doom" or another. Throughout history men have prematurely prepared the church's tombstone. But God's church won't die. She has been mighty sick of late, but do not think for one moment she is in danger of passing away . . . not of natural causes!

All those who predict extinction forget one thing: the recuperative capacity of the church. Remember, the church is the body of Christ. It is indwelt by his Spirit. For the church to die, the Spirit must expire or cease to work. But, to the contrary, it just so happens that part of the Spirit's ministry on earth is resuscitative (1 Pet. 3:18). The Spirit quickens to life and revives: "But if the Spirit of him that raised up Jesus from the dead dwell in you, he that raised up Christ from the dead shall also quicken your mortal bodies by his Spirit that dwelleth in you" (Rom. 8:11).

In time, that ever-present Spirit quickens to new life and makes us equal to the demands of our ever-changing world! In fact, the church is passing through the early stages of spiritual renewal at this time. The evidence is undeniable. Invariably, when people experience the reality of God in their lives, their immediate response is to offer themselves for God's use. The journey into usefulness begins!

For example, Ezekiel's valley of dry bones experienced new life. First, the bones came together; sinews then came upon the bones; flesh upon the sinews; skin over the flesh; and finally they received the fresh breath of life. But what we so often fail to notice is that when these bones came alive, they stood up on their feet, assembled as "an exceeding great army" ready to carry out the orders of their commander (Ezek. 37:10).

When Isaiah encountered God and saw him "high and lifted up," he repented of his sin. Then, after his sin was purged, he could hear the voice of his Lord saying, "Whom shall I send, and who will go for us?" And Isaiah responded, "Here am I; send me" (Isa. 6:8). And when Paul finally encountered Christ on the Damascus road, his response was the same: "Lord, what wilt thou have me to do?" (Acts 9:6).

That's it. The response never varies. *The clearest evidence of spiritual renewal will always be a Christian saying: "Lord, what wilt thou have me to do?"* This is the sign of renewal.

This is a sign of our time. It is precisely what we are witnessing today. Christian laymen by the thousands have experienced genuine spiritual renewal, and they are stepping forth to inquire, "What would God have me do?"

These laymen, their lives aglow with God, wanting a mission in life, hail the prospect of a new day in the church. For we are finally grasping the concept that has been in God's mind from the beginning. A *ministering laity* has always been God's plan of service. This is the revolutionary biblical concept that will eventually transform the church of tomorrow. A "spirit-enthused" laity journeying forth to minister . . . on mission for Christ.

Now, to grasp the revolutionary aspect of this concept, you must place the emphasis upon the second word of this phrase, a "ministering *laity*." The word *laity* is derived from the Greek word *laos*. It refers to "the people of God." Laity, then, has reference to Christians in general, as over against pastors or those serving in full-time church-related vocations. Therefore, a ministering laity means the "Lord's work" will be carried out by all church members.

Each Christian is a minister. This was God's original strategy. It was reborn in the Reformation. Martin Luther apparently introduced this principle, which he called the "priesthood of the believer," on Christmas Day, 1520.[1] But it has just now come of age. The church is finally learning to place the responsibility of ministry squarely where God placed it . . . upon the people who occupy the pews. Carlyle Marney said: "The church you have known all your lives with its intensely dominant and active minister and a passively supporting laity is not God's people in this world: not any more." [2] God will make no more giants; now it is time to elevate the race!

The hottest thing going within the Christian camp today is the rekindled hope of thousands who envision a greater church tomorrow . . . because laymen everywhere have "come alive" in Spirit-filled service. Thousands of laymen have "entered the ministry" in the truest sense of this word. Elton Trueblood has said, "The theory and practice of the *lay ministry* has been the greatest single work of emerging vitality in the church of the twentieth century." [3]

Oh, this is not to imply that everyone will embrace this new role "that the ministry belongs to the laity." Not on your life!

Many *laymen* don't want it. That's what they "bought" their preacher for: to do what laymen can't; to do what laymen don't want to. And the laymen are not alone in rejecting the concept of "lay ministry." Many *preachers* don't want it. As someone said, "After all, who else can gallop out of the house seven days out of every week, deserting home and family, and still be admired by all for his devotion to the 'ministry'?"

Neither is this to say that each and every church congregation will experience this rejuvenated lay membership. Not every congregation will withstand the ebb tides of secularism. Indeed, many congregations will dwindle away. But some believe the Laodicean church of Revelation characterizes the lukewarm condition of churches in the last days of history. And the Bible indicates God will have his "overcomers" even then! (See Rev. 3:21.)

Therefore, let us examine this concept of a "ministering laity." Let's take a three-dimensional look at it. That is, we will discuss it from a biblical, practical, and historical point of view.

Lay Ministry from a Biblical Perspective

"Renewal" as the word is used today refers to an idea, *the recovery of a New Testament concept:* that all believers are to be ministers, and the pastor's duty is to "train the ministers" (Eph. 4:12). (And the best *method* of training Christians to minister might well be the small-group approach, which will be discussed in our last chapter.)

David Haney has written three masterful books on the subject of the small-group approach which are destined to be handbooks for the church of tomorrow. In his latest book, *Breakthrough into Renewal,* Dr. Haney states as the basic premise of the renewal movement: "that the church will be renewed in our time only as the laity become ministers." [4]

In another book, *The Idea of the Laity,* Dr. Haney again trumpets this truth:

> Those committed to Christ's church and to its renewal in our time are also committed to a basic premise: that renewal will come only as we successfully activate the laity. The activation and development of the vast lay resources is priority business for the church today simply because they are intrinsic to authentic Christianity. *Biblically speaking,* the laity . . . *are* the "ministers" of Christ. Not "pastors," mind you, but "ministers." [5]

Writing with typical clarity and conciseness, Dr. Haney observes that "somewhere between A.D. 33 and the present, 'minister' moved both grammatically and theologically from a verb (a thing done) to a noun (a person doing it): what was originally a *function of* the church became a *station in* the church." [6]

How true! When we use the word *minister* today, we usually have reference to an officer of the church, a pastor. But the biblical meaning of the word *minister* has reference to something done . . . a service rendered. The pastor is to perfect (equip or train) the saints "for the work of the ministry" (Eph. 4:12). So, scripturally speaking, the ministry is every Christian's job!

Lay Ministry from a Practical Perspective

The choice analogy of a profile which indicates the ideal project-to-people ratio of a church program is a *pyramid:*

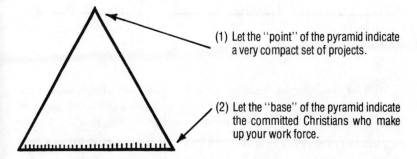

(1) Let the "point" of the pyramid indicate a very compact set of projects.

(2) Let the "base" of the pyramid indicate the committed Christians who make up your work force.

Such a profile points out the need for a broad base of support for a clearly defined endeavor. The triangular shape accentuates this ideal of a large work force functioning up and through a compact, limited set of objectives.

Obviously, to maintain this profile, the work force which forms your base of support should be increased simultaneously and proportionately with added projects. In most churches, however, it seems that various additional projects have been added at the top to widen the spearhead of objectives—without an equivalent broadening of the base of support. Perhaps the missions committee organizes two mission outreach projects, the Brotherhood enlarges its boys' program, the building committee begins a building enlargement campaign, the choir triples its program of tours and concerts, the Women's Missionary Society organizes a series of auxiliary projects, and the youth program comes alive and breaks out with a rash of projects that requires additional parental and sponsor involvement.

As these and other projects are added, the profile begins to expand at the top . . . precariously.

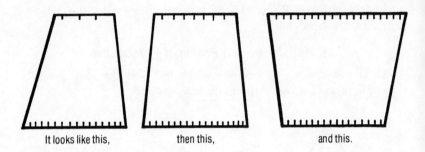

It looks like this,   then this,   and this.

And let this process continue for a few years, and the least of consequences is a top-heavy program with an inadequate work force of people who are too "pooped" to be potent.

However, the greater consequence is when our top line of projects so swamps the basic work force that people grow tired and quit. We lose workers rather than maintain our base of support. And as our committed workers decrease, the profile of our program can actually resemble an inverted pyramid. (See p. 17.)

Our church program is upside-down. And the church staff runs wildly up and down the top line, like a juggler with his line of plates spinning on poles, attempting to keep each one from falling off.

The only hope for effectively increasing the ministries of our local churches is to enlarge the number of committed laymen who make up the work force of the local churches.

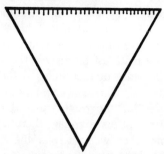

Lay Ministry from an Historical Perspective

Christians are still passive; there is a "Master's Minority" of devoted followers regrouping for renewal all across the land. Our churches still must offer everything from "free" bus rides to "green stamps" in order to get the masses to attend Sunday School. On the other hand, there is a growing nucleus of people hungry for spiritual growth. They are complaining that one hour on Sunday is insufficient. So they gather in small groups. They meet in homes . . . on week nights . . . for several hours of additional fellowship, prayer, and study of the Word. These groups are springing up all over the world. David Haney identifies this small-group phenomena as the work of God in our day: "Its unplanned-ness is seen in the fact that no denomination had either schedule or strategy for it and, to date, most have done little to implement it. This spontaneity bears all the earmarks of a moving of the Spirit . . . who usually operates from the church's blindside." [7]

Within church congregations throughout the world, representing most every denominational affiliation, there is spiritual renewal among some of the people, the beginning of a movement so significant that Jack Taylor exclaimed: "I am under the awesome impression that we are on the verge of the greatest Spirit-visitation since the beginning of Christendom." [8] Perhaps this is an overstatement, but some of our churches are in for renewal—because God is up to something!

Our laymen are experiencing the reality of the Holy Spirit's power, *and they know the Spirit's empowering is for service.* If we spiritually cultivate our inner life without any consideration of outward service, all we have is a kind of "hothouse" religion. Discriminating pastors are seeking to equip their laymen for Spirit-empowered service.

A revolution is breaking out within the church. Some laymen want to be more deeply involved in the spiritual ministries of the church. They want to do more than just help serve the "Supper." Rightly so! As Huxley said, "The sense of uselessness is the severest shock that any organism can sustain." Christian laymen have suffered that shock because "doing chores for the pastor around the church just isn't enough." They are tired of just standing there as pillars for our half-supported institutions. They want part of the action . . . they long for God to accomplish things of eternal significance through *their* lives. Many have discovered the joy in being redemptively used of God to bless others. They are catching the spirit of their Savior who "came not to be served but to serve" (see Mark 10:45). In short, they want to get off the bench and get into the game!

This will require more involvement from the pew in our worship services, more instructional preaching from the pulpit. We will *gather* to *scatter.* That is, we gather and minister to one another for spiritual refreshment and renewal . . . all in order to scatter throughout our world in service as a witness of Him. We gather to share our victories and worship our God, to recoup and regroup for the coming week of service. It is this common objective, by the way, that binds us together in the highest experience of Christian fellowship.

Real fellowship is derived from unity in a common objective and is experienced only by those jointly engaged in that common effort. This was the import of Trueblood's dictum: "Profound fellowship is always *directional* in origin; it comes from looking together in the same direction." [9] Therefore, Christians, bound together in Spirit-empowered service of a common Lord, enjoy fellowship in its highest expression.

It is this directional fellowship—Christians bound together in Spirit-empowered service of a common Lord—that will revitalize some churches against the ominous threat of extinction in a secularistic society and maintain some congregations through the intense ostracism and intolerance of tomorrow. For, as the world grows more non-Christian, some churches will become more Christian, paradoxical as that may seem. Our secularistic world will grow more *intolerant,* then become outright *antagonistic* toward the evangelical church. However, persecution in any form can serve to purify the church and rid her of the uncommitted. The committed will cross the line and stay at it until Jesus comes!

So, God intends to use the persecution which will characterize the last days: "He will sift out everything without solid foundations, so that only unshakable things will be left" (Heb. 12:27, TLB). A purer bride will greet her coming Lord. And the Bible definitely states that the emphasis in such a day ought to be upon *service:* "Wherefore we receiving a kingdom which cannot be moved, let us have grace whereby we may *serve God acceptably* with reverance and godly fear" (Heb. 12:28, italics added).

Furthermore, as I have said, the clearest evidence of that renewal is a Christian saying: "Lord, what will thou have me do?" This book provides some guidelines for that journey into usefulness . . . as you seek to *find and follow God's will for your life!*

Notes

1. Earnest G. Schwiebert, *Luther and His Times* (St. Louis: Concordia Publishing House, 1950), p. 443.

2. Carlyle Marney, *Priests to Each Other* (Valley Forge: Judson Press, 1974), p. 14.

3. Elton Trueblood, *The Future of the Christian,* (New York: Harper and Row, 1971), p. 28.

4. David P. Haney, *Breakthrough into Renewal* (Nashville: Broadman Press, 1974), p. 22.

5. David P. Haney, *The Idea of the Laity* (Grand Rapids, Michigan: Zondervan, 1973), pp. 21-22.

6. *Ibid.*, p. 40.

7. Haney, *Idea of the Laity*, p. 53.

8. Jack Taylor, *Much More* (Nashville: Broadman Press, 1972), p. 160.

9. Trueblood, p. 51.

2
God Leads—by Way of Calvary

Genuine spiritual renewal always raises one distinctive question: "How do I find and follow God's will for my life?"

The most practical answer to this question is a pivotal statement embedded deep in the book of Romans. It is the central statement in all the New Testament concerning God's guidance of your life.

> I beseech you therefore brethren, by the mercies of God, that ye present your bodies a living sacrifice, holy, acceptable unto God, which is your reasonable service. And be not conformed to this world: but be ye transformed by the renewing of your mind *that ye may prove what is that good, and acceptable, and perfect, will of God* (Rom. 12:12, italics added).

These two verses will form our key passage and serve as the anchor to which everything I say will be tied. This book is but an amplification and elaboration of all these two verses imply in terms of finding and following God's will.

To begin with, examine what our key passage actually promises. Isolate the last phrase. It definitely states you *can* know God's will: "That you may prove what is that good, and acceptable, and perfect, will of God." But it also flatly declares that God's will is *worth* knowing. It is "good"—everything in God's plan is good for you; it is "acceptable"—God will never expect too much of you (at times you might think he has); and it is "perfect"—the very best plan for your life.

God's will can be known; it is worth knowing; and the Scriptures elsewhere declare you are responsible for knowing that will. "Wherefore be ye not unwise, but understanding what the will of the Lord is" (Eph. 5:17). Begin by examining what our text tells you to do in order to find and follow God's will. For there is only one way into God's perfect will for your life. The main road begins at Calvary . . . as you enter a life of sacrifice for others and take up your own personal cross.

The Way of Calvary . . . an Exposition

The initial verse of our central passage sets forth the *first prerequisite* for finding and following God's will. It stipulates in a half-sentence the basis upon which God guides your life: "that ye present your bodies a living sacrifice, holy, acceptable unto God, which is your reasonable service" (Rom. 12:1).

In all of Paul's writings, perhaps there is never a verse in which he packs more informative instruction into one, compact half-sentence. The central word is *sacrifice.* God's fundamental call to each Christian is nothing less than the sacrifice of one's life for others. Analyze the above half-sentence. Dissect it like an eagle-eyed newspaper correspondent would search through it, asking the following questions:

1. Sacrifice *what?* God said to "present your bodies a living sacrifice." The "body" is specified because it includes all you are: hands, feet, mind, lips, conscience, emotions, and will.

When God balances his books and calls you to account for your life as a Christian, this is what you will be held accountable for. You will be rewarded on the basis of what you have done with your body: "For we must all appear before the judgment seat of Christ; that every one may receive the things done in his *body,* according to that he hath done" (2 Cor. 5:10, italics added). Your body is "what" you sacrifice.

2. Sacrifice *when?* God said you are to "*present* your bodies a *living* sacrifice." In the original Greek, the verb *present* is in the aorist tense. This means to present it *once and for all.* On the other hand, you are to present it as a "living" sacrifice, and the word *living* denotes a perpetual activity. Taken together, these two words indicate you make a once-and-for-all decision (burning the bridges behind you) to enter a life-style of forever living your life as a sacrifice for others!

Stephen Olford tells of a lady approaching him at the close of a service to say: "All this business about consecration and surrender is sheer nonsense. It does not work. I have tried it several times, and it just won't work." Dr. Olford thought she was in need of a firm rebuke, so he replied, "My friend, you have lied to God and to me, for I know you have never truly sacrificed your life." Rather shaken, she begged him to explain. "New Testament surrender," he said, "is not a matter of a day, a week, a month, or a year. It is a contract for life. If you say you have sacrificed your life, *what are you doing off the altar?*" [1]

3. Sacrifice *where?* Our text says we are to present our bodies in "service" and "unto God." The word for service speaks of spiritual service and reflects the Old Testament concept of sacrificial offerings (see Heb. 9:6). You are to sacrifice yourself unto God.

Of course, doing this for others is the only way you can actually do anything for God. He has no needs. It is only as you do things for those he loves that you can do something for him. The Bible pictures a great commendation day. The Kingdom saints will be rewarded for feeding Christ when he was hungry and thirsty, for offering him shelter when he was a stranger, for clothing him when he was naked, and for visiting him when he was sick and in prison.

Incredulously, they will inquire: "Lord, when saw we thee an hungred, and fed thee? or thirsty, and gave thee drink? When saw we thee a stranger, and took thee in? or naked, and clothed thee? Or when saw we thee sick, or in prison, and came unto thee?" (Matt. 25:37-39).

Jesus shall answer, "Verily I say unto you, *Inasmuch as ye have done it unto one of the least of these my brethren, ye have done it unto me*" (Matt. 25:40, italics added). We give ourselves for others as a service unto God . . . that is "where" we sacrifice.

4. Sacrifice *why?* God said to present your bodies . . . because it is "your *reasonable* service." It is the logic of love: "The very spring of our actions is the love of Christ. We look at it like this: If one died for all men then, in a sense, they all died, and his purpose in dying for them is that their lives now should be no longer lived for themselves but for him who died . . . for them" (2 Cor. 5:14-15, Phillips). It is unthinkable, from the standpoint of the cross, that we would do any less. It is your reasonable service . . . that is "why" you sacrifice.

5. Sacrifice *how?* God said the sacrifice must be *"holy,* acceptable unto God." A holy sacrifice is one which is totally consecrated or set apart unto him . . . which means you must be set apart *from* some-

thing—your self-will—and set apart *to* something—his will. That is "how" you sacrifice.

To sum up our exposition, you make a once-and-for-all decision to enter a life-style to forever sacrifice (when) . . . your body (what) . . . for others as a service unto God (where) . . . setting yourself apart from your own self-will to do his will (how) . . . as your reasonable service of love (why).

This is actually another way of stating the fundamental demand of Christ: "If any man will come after me, let him deny himself, and take up his cross daily, and follow me" (Luke 9:23).

There is some confusion, however, about what Jesus meant by "take up your cross." For instance, your cross has nothing to do with the hardship you incur in the course of your daily existence. Your cross is *what you suffer in the process of serving others.* The cross of Jesus was a *vicarious* cross. By vicarious I mean Jesus died *on behalf of others.* Therefore, to take up his cross is to live *vicariously.* Your cross has reference to the difficulty you incur while denying yourself in service to others.

So, the demand is always the same. If you want to find and follow God's will for your life, you must deny your self-will, take up your cross of service to others daily, and follow Christ.

Of course, then the underlying *principle* behind this first requirement is that God guides the obedient. God's will is revealed as you are willing to obey it, willing to the point of *sacrificing* your life for others as Christ gave his life on the cross. God always leads . . . by the way of Calvary.

The Way of Calvary . . . an Example

I once took an automobile trip which has become quite meaningful to me. I have thought of it often as an example of the manner in which a Christian discovers God's will for his life. It was Friday evening. My family and I were driving part of the night from one conference to another. The highway was long and lonely, and my mind began to dwell on certain aspects of travel which I had always taken for granted. Here we were, driving to a place I had never been. I did not know if the roads ahead would be rough or smooth, narrow or wide, straight or curved. I had no way of knowing if a bridge were out, where traffic would be heaviest, where speed limits varied, or what areas would have detours because of repair. This is not to mention the impossibility of forecasting weather conditions which might affect my journey.

Nevertheless, I started my car, turned on my headlights, and drove off into the night. Now there is an interesting thing about the headlights of an automobile . . . they provide only enough light for the road just ahead. There is no way of seeing all the route at one time. However, my headlights pierced the darkness to reveal the road ahead and illumined each highway sign as I approached it. And the signs were more than adequate to warn me of the curves, stops, crossroads, and detours.

As I drove along that night, I suddenly became conscious that my basic underlying attitude was one of *confident faith*. It never even occurred to me that we would fail to reach our destination. After all, I had enough light to navigate the road ahead. Higher authorities had marked the highway before me . . . and the further I traveled, the further my lights would shine!

Now, I want you to envision that car as it journeyed through the night with its lights illuminating the road. Perhaps more than any similar example, this experience suggests to me the most important factor concerning God's guidance of a Christian life. With rare exceptions, God's guiding lights are much like the headlights of that car . . . God reveals just enough light for the road ahead. That is, God reveals just enough light for your immediate future only; *but the further you follow, the more light you receive.* I call it the "Commander Principle": to the extent in which you have obeyed God's wishes as commands, to that degree God reveals his will for your life. This is the import of a passage in John which states: "If any man will do his will, he shall know" (John 7:17).

If you are honestly willing to do God's will, you *can* know it. The most important question, then, regarding the discovery of God's will for your life has to do with obedience: *Are you obedient to as much of God's will as you know right now?* That is the question! Just as in our example: Your car lights shine further only as you progress down the road! In the very same sense, God will reveal more of his will when you are doing all you know to do of his will right now!

To me, the fact of limited spiritual foresight was a revelation. For I had always thought that if you were deeply "spiritually-minded," God would give you some type of vision with regard to your *future destiny* . . . so you could understand all that was happening along the way. I saw God much like our modern helicopter traffic controller, who hovers in flight over many of our major cities each day. From his *perspective* high in the sky, this airborne traffic controller can see all the major arteries as they fan out over the city. He can see the overall pattern of traffic flow. He can spot congested areas and traffic jams. He explains delays and suggests the quickest route, he reports on accidents. And he broadcasts all this information to each and every automobile which contains a radio . . . whose driver will tune in on the proper wavelength.

Yes, it was once my impression that you could find God's will in this manner. As if God would reveal the total picture to the spiritually elite . . . those who had faith enough to tune in on his wavelength. Therefore, I wasted a great deal of time looking into the providential purpose of the events going on around me. I assumed an ability to understand why God had done what he had done in each particular case (and what he would do next). I found myself pondering over providence . . . attempting to read a message about God's secret purposes out of every unusual thing that happened. I thought it was my responsibility to take each significant experience as a sign for some type of response on my part.

J. I. Packer exposed the folly of this way of thinking. His remarks were brief and to the point, but I saw myself in every line. For example, he said that we often claim such inside information as to all the why and wherefore of God's doings *for His honor* (and also, though we do not say this, for the sake of our own reputation as "spiritual" Christians). We mistakenly assume it is a mark of maturity to have all the answers, so this pretense becomes a part of us.

> We feel sure that God has enabled us to understand all His ways with us and our circle thus far, and we take it for granted that we shall be able to see at once the reason for anything that may happen to us in the future. And then something very painful and quite inexplicable

comes along and our cheerful illusion of being in on God's secret council is shattered. Our pride is wounded; we feel that God has slighted us and unless at this point we repent and humble ourselves very thoroughly for our former presumptions, our whole subsequent spiritual life might be blighted.[2]

The truth is that God has hidden from us *most* everything we would like to know about his providential purposes. He does so both to keep us humble and to teach us to walk by faith. The ways of the Spirit are beyond us: "Just as you can hear the wind but can't tell where it comes from or where it will go next, so it is with the Spirit" (John 3:8, TLB).

This has certainly been true in my life. The Holy Spirit has led me from one thing to another . . . without my having the slightest idea what he was doing at the time. Nothing has happened like I would have planned it. I had not anticipated any graduate work beyond my first seminary degree, certainly not my twelve years as a pastor on the "pioneer" fields of my denomination's outreach, or my return to a great church in Texas, or the itinerant teaching ministry that is mine today. You do God's will without realizing it . . . as God gives you enough insight for the road just ahead of you.

After all, when you are driving an automobile, it is the *response quotient* (obedience) that counts. The quickness of your reaction to that which is asked of you . . . that is the most important factor. You don't ask yourself why that zigzag is in the road just where it is, as if that is to have some providential meaning. *You simply concentrate on maneuvering correctly.* "To live wisely," counsels Dr. Packer, "you have to be clear-sighted and realistic—ruthlessly so—in looking at life as it is."

No, God doesn't reveal his will from the unlimited perspective of a helicopter, high above the city. Finding and following God's will is more like driving across the country . . . at night. And you receive more light only as you travel down the road.

Furthermore, the underlying reason you receive more light only as you travel down the road is that there is a *sequence* in which God wants you to discover and experience his will. Only those who obey God's *first* wishes are ready to experience higher guidance. And, as set forth in Romans 12:1, the *first* prerequisite for finding God's will is to "present your body a living sacrifice," or as Jesus expressed it: "If any man will come after me, let him deny himself, and take up his cross daily, and follow me" (Luke 9:23). *"Take up your cross"* . . . this is your first step in following Christ, and the main road into God's will.

But there is also a *deeper* reason—inherent in the very nature of guidance itself—that necessitates a call away from yourself and into service . . . as a prerequisite for discovering God's will. For it is only as you lose yourself in service to others that you will be able to understand God's perfect plan for your life.

We all share the same great difficulty in discovering God's will. We have an "I" problem. We are so blinded by our own selfish desires that we fail to see God's will for our lives.

Indeed, "self-ism" is the very essence of sin. Sin is the putting of one's own selfish will, the *self-will,* in opposition to the will of God. It is doing what self desires instead of doing what God wills.

Therefore, God *reverses* your self-centered inclinations by giving you a mission in life in service to others. Your cross is what you do for others!

The first thing God wants of each Christian is a *ministry* (service). Every disciple has received at least this much "light" . . . and you will receive little in-depth guidance until you begin to live for others, as unto God. As I see it, to "present your bodies a living sacrifice" is the same thing as saying, "Deny yourself, take up your cross, and follow Christ." This is the way of Calvary. And this is the way into God's will.

The Way of Calvary . . . an Experience

While writing this, I had occasion to counsel with a young married man whose life was typical of so many with whom I have spoken. He had made a commitment to Jesus Christ as Lord and Savior of his life. And that initial commitment was followed by a time of exhilarating joy and consuming devotion. He began to study the Bible with relish and experienced some times of real enjoyment in prayer. He attended church with regularity. And the moral tone of his life experienced an immediate change for the better.

However, his Christian life never developed beyond this first "baby" stage. That is, he never developed beyond the stage of *receiving* from others . . . to the point where God could begin *giving* to others through him.

Therefore, several years later, his relationship with Christ lost its freshness. He still attended church, but he became much less enthusiastic about the Christian way of life. He seldom "got into" his Bible and felt far too removed from God to pray very often. He was experiencing ever-increasing degrees of spiritual defeat. And his mind was laden with deep guilt over repeated lapses into sin. Having found it impossible to exercise consistent discipline with regard to things he knew to be wrong, he soon found himself going around in circles trying to do something about it. He had lost all real sense of direction for his life. He asked me point-blank, "How do you find and follow God's will for your life?"

Fortunately, after hours of conversation together, God provided some spiritual illumination and enabled me to drive home one basic suggestion. I suggested that he climb up and out of the slippery pit of morbid introspection, take his eyes off himself, and begin to think in terms

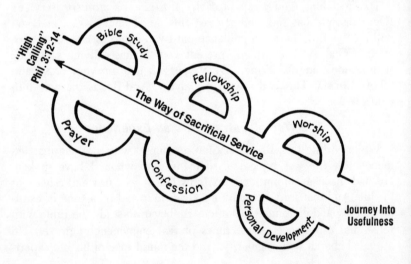

of what God would like to do through him for others. I used a simple diagram which made all the difference in that young man's life—as it has to others. Picture the main road of Christian living as one of service to others, and various other aspects as side roads, somewhat like the roadside parks which you find along our highways. The way of service is the *main* road; the other roads are for temporary refreshment.

The problem comes when we Christians get *sidetracked* by a preoccupation with our own self-enrichment. We compulsively turn aside. Consequently, we lose all sense of direction. We cease to progress along the road of Christian service *and find ourselves running around in one (or more) of several circles,* as illustrated below:

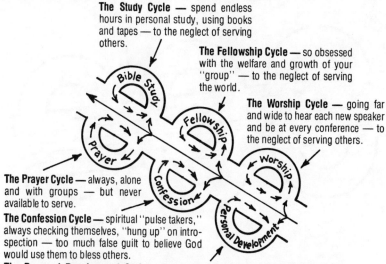

The Study Cycle — spend endless hours in personal study, using books and tapes — to the neglect of serving others.

The Fellowship Cycle — so obsessed with the welfare and growth of your "group" — to the neglect of serving the world.

The Worship Cycle — going far and wide to hear each new speaker and be at every conference — to the neglect of serving others.

The Prayer Cycle — always, alone and with groups — but never available to serve.

The Confession Cycle — spiritual "pulse takers," always checking themselves, "hung up" on introspection — too much false guilt to believe God would use them to bless others.

The Personal Development Cycle — sees all as a glorified "self-improvement course," so busy concentrating on eating properly, physical exercise, personal grooming, expanding the mind, keeping up with fashions, news, recreation, etc. — has no time for service to others.

Such cycles remind me of the boy at the fair who spent all his dimes on the merry-go-round, to which his brother disgustedly remarked, "There you is—you spent all you had; you got off where you got on, and you ain't been nowhere!"

However—concerning the young man we counseled—once he took

up his cross and developed a life-style which centered in sacrificial service to others, *everything else began to fall in place.* This is basic. Once sacrificial Christian service becomes the priority of your life, all the other "side road" activities will become a real source of spiritual refreshment, as God intended.

Your devotional time, your worship and praise, your fellowship, your cleansing, your personal development are all for the purpose of strengthening your life for the service of your Lord, as a blessing to others.

Let's take one more look at our last visual analogy. Notice the many arrows which point downward . . . while the road of service leads upward.

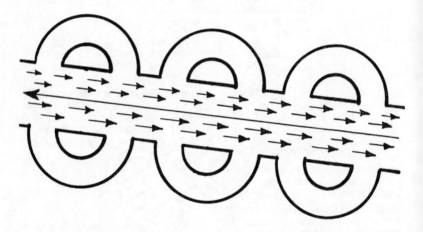

The Bible speaks of two main roads of life. The way of "selfishness" is a *broad road* through a wide gate . . . with *heavy traffic.* To the contrary, the way of "service" is depicted as a *narrow road* through a small gate . . . and is *comparatively untraveled* (see Matt. 7:13-14).

I used to have a false picture of those two roads. People would speak of straying *off* the "straight and narrow." So, I always pictured a straight and narrow road with endless highways veering off to the right or left. Then a better analogy caught my eye, and I believe the

Bible really pictures it like this: the heavier traffic is on the broad road because it leads *downhill*. It is most easily traveled, but it leads downward to destruction—not only destruction in eternity, but destruction of self, purpose, and meaning in this life.

And what about the narrow road? The narrow road is gained by repentance (turning to go in the other direction), and it leads right back up through the middle of the broad road in the *opposite* direction. It is uphill and counter-flowing, against the current of humanity. Therefore, no one will just naturally drift in this direction. It is hard going—uphill all the way. Christ bore his cross up Calvary's hill. And when a Christian takes up his cross to follow Christ, he does not merely turn back onto a straight and narrow path. Rather, he turns and makes his way *back up the center of life's broad road, in the opposite direction*. He will come into constant conflict with those who would oppose the things he stands for.

But there is much to be gained by traveling the road of service to others. For it is just such service that will most quickly bring you to the end of yourself, as you discover the absolute futility of attempting to serve God in your own strength and ability. And the discovery of your inadequacy should lead you into a Spirit-filled (empowered) life.

Furthermore, the endless conflicts you encounter by "bucking the crowd" and going against the course of this world will be used of God like "heavenly sandpaper" to smooth off the rough spots in your life.

Difficulty but provides you with traction for your upward climb. Satanic stumbling blocks become stepping-stones. And those side roads, as pictured in our illustration, begin to take on their proper significance. Bible study, prayer, confession, fellowship, worship, and personal development all find their fulfillment in refreshing you along the road of service.

Furthermore, just as service is the *first* road into God's will, there is also a *specific route* of service to which God will direct each and every Christian. That is, there is a specific way in which God will most effectively use your life. The Bible refers to this as your "spiritual gift" for service . . . for it is a God-given way for your life to best count for him.

Several chapters will be devoted to finding your spiritual gift—

because it is only those who make it this far on the journey to whom God reveals his will in the fullest sense. This is your *first* major goal as a Christian. It is Route #1 for your life!

Notes

1. Stephen F. Olford, *I'll Take the High Road* (Grand Rapids: Zondervan Publishing House, 1969), p. 31.

2. J. I. Packer, *Knowing God* (Downers Grove, Illinois: Inter-Varsity Press, 1973), p. 95.

3

The Timothy Temperament

The main road into God's will is a *service road*, and traffic is on the increase. But the rate of traffic flow would multiply if we could rid ourselves of one major roadblock.

Christians share a common reluctance about serving God. And their objection is always stated somewhat like this: *"But I just can't see how God could use someone like me!"* Somehow our Christian training has left many of us with such low self-esteem that we are unable to believe God could use us. We are timid. We are handicapped by what I choose to call a "Timothy Temperament."

Our Difficulty Is Timidity

Timothy had a weakness of temperament. He was extremely timid. The apostle Paul recognized this disposition in him and felt led of God to write about it in his second letter to Timothy. So I want to take a detailed look at the epistle of 2 Timothy with this in mind. Indeed, the conditions of that time so parallel our own that the similarity is unmistakable.

First, in the days when 2 Timothy was written, the spiritual condition was grave. The Neronian persecution was on the increase. Heresy was setting in. And there was an almost total Asian apostasy from Paul's teaching (2 Tim. 1:15). Paul actually wrote the letter from a prison cell. Bishop Moule appraised the situation as critical: "Christianity . . . trembled, *humanly speaking,* on the verge of annihilation." [1]

You can be certain, then, Paul was writing with measured words. And how significant that the *first* thing Paul said was to remind Timothy about the importance of his spiritual gift for service. Doesn't this say something to us about the urgent need to exercise our service gifts in this age of spiritual apostasy?

In his first letter to Timothy, Paul had said: "Neglect not the gift that is in thee" (1 Tim. 4:14). The word *neglect* is in the present imperative, a prohibition in Greek grammar that forbids the continuance of an act already going on. Paul was telling Timothy to stop neglecting his spiritual gift because Timothy was, as a matter of fact, doing just that. Therefore, in his second letter to Timothy, Paul is telling him to activate the gift of God when he says: "Wherefore . . . *stir up* the gift of God, which is in thee" (2 Tim. 1:6, italics added). Having issued this command to Timothy, Paul immediately states the reason for this exhortation: "For God did not give us a spirit of *timidity*" (2 Tim. 1:7, RSV and Amplified).

A basic flaw had developed in the temperament of Timothy. It hindered him in terms of Christian service. Timothy evidently shrank from difficult tasks. So, in writing to the Corinthians, Paul had to pave the way for his mission: "When Timothy comes, see that you put him at ease among you" (1 Cor. 16:10-11). John Stott says that Timothy was shy: "He appears to have been a very shy and sensitive creature, to whom responsibility was an onerous burden. Perhaps he was also fearful of spiritual excesses and extravagances. So Paul is obliged not only to urge him to keep stirring up his gift but to reassure him that he need not be diffident about exercising it." [2] Stott also quotes Patrick Fairbairn as saying Timothy was "disposed to lean rather than to lead." [3]

But Timothy's temperament has reached epidemic proportions in our day, and it can be evidenced in every conference where a serious attempt is made at helping Christians find God's will for their lives in terms of service. *It is very hard to discover something you are not looking for!* And some of us find it hard to give any serious consideration to the idea that we can be of service to God.

Somehow it feels presumptuous to claim an ability to minister, especially when it is not even easy for us to think good thoughts about ourselves. The fact is that most of us are blind to our positive attributes. We have a hang-up about thinking we can be used of God . . . a Timothy Temperament!

Bruce Larson and Ralph Osborne have a simple demonstration they use in conferences to reveal this inner negative bias—this inferiority complex—this low self-esteem. Bruce Larson mentions this technique in *two* of his books. The following is one account of the test:

> Take a piece of notebook paper and jot down five words which symbolize for you five different qualities or characteristics which you do not like about yourself and which you wish were different. Time yourself to see how long it takes to do this. Then, on another piece of paper, write down five words which symbolize five qualities or characteristics which are your strengths. Time yourself in writing these five words. Which took longer? [4]

Larson reports that, regardless of what kind of people attempt this exercise, the majority will list their negatives within forty seconds. But the same group will still be trying to list their positives after a minute and a half, with two minutes not unusual. Somehow our Christian training has made us more conscious of our liabilities than our assets! This is why some of us are unlikely to get serious about serving God until we can break through our guilt and find enough faith to believe we really can be used in service!

Our Disposition Can Be Transformed

The real value of this recognition of our difficulty and the identification of it as a Timothy Temperament is that Paul assured Timothy he could overcome his timidity; Paul told him what to do about it. And this transformation is still possible today.

First, Paul gave Timothy some assurance: "Hence I remind you to rekindle the gift of God that is within you . . . *for God did not give us a spirit of timidity but a spirit of power and love and self-control* (2 Tim. 1:6-7, RSV, italics added). In these italicized words, Paul is making reference to the Holy Spirit, whom all Christians (note he says "us") have received. Paul is emphasizing how the Holy Spirit can help to overcome the paralysis of our self-demeaning timidity. As I see it, Paul is speaking of a cycle, or a chain reaction. The Holy Spirit provides: power, then love, then a sound mind—*in that order*. And this sequence of events will occur something like this: (1) Once the Holy Spirit has significantly demonstrated his liberating *power* in your life, (2) he can then flood your heart with a deep assurance of God's love, (3) which, in turn, quickens your faith and you become sound of mind, realizing God can and will use someone like you. No longer will you need an exhortation to "stir up" your gift. (This cycle will be seen again, in more detail, in chapter 5). You will be eager to serve!

So the one question remains: how do you set off this cycle? What releases the fullness of God's power in your life and triggers this chain reaction?

Later in 2 Timothy, Paul tells us what to do in order to initiate this sequence of experiences in the Holy Spirit. In so doing, Paul put his finger on the one basic requirement of effective Christian service. The one vital prerequisite for service in general, and a spiritual gift in particular, is a *consecrated* life.

> In a great house there are not only vessels of gold and silver but also of wood and earthenware, some for noble use, some for ignoble. If any one purifies himself from what is ignoble, then he will be a vessel for noble use, *consecrated* and useful to the master of the house, ready for any good work. (2 Tim. 2:20-21, RSV, italics added)

A consecrated life is God's requirement for fruitful Christian service. The passage assures us that such a servant will be "a vessel for noble use," "useful to the master," and "ready for any good work."

But what is a "consecrated" life? The word consecrated means *to be set apart without sin for God's use of your life*. You do so by *"purifying"* it: "If anyone purifies himself . . . then he will be . . . consecrated" (2 Tim. 2:21, RSV). The Master lays down one condition for the vessel he uses: it must be clean! Therefore, to consecrate your life you must purify it—a truth which is further confirmed by the fact that this teaching is sandwiched between two clear allusions to personal holiness: "Let every one who names the name of the Lord depart from iniquity" (vs. 19) and "so shun youthful passions and aim at righteousness" (vs. 22). We get to the bottom of your need when we ask, "How do you purify your life in order to consecrate it?"

Our Duty Will Be Two-fold

A pure (consecrated) heart will necessitate both *negative* and *positive* action: "*Flee* also youthful lusts: but *follow* after righteousness . . .

out of a *pure* heart" (2 Tim. 2:22, italics added). Do you see what is being said here? Purity results from both a negative action (flee) and a positive one (follow). Notice the sharp contrast between these two verbs. *Flee* (Greek *pheugo*) means to *escape*. *Follow* (Greek *dioko*) is the exact opposite, and it means to *pursue* or *chase*.

To consecrate your life, you purify it—which is a two-fold task. You escape from the "lusts" of the old nature *and* pursue righteousness. As in the case of Israel in the Old Testament, you escape from Egypt *and* pursue your Promised Land. As Peter expressed it: "You escape the corruption that is in the world through lust," *that* "ye might be partakers of the divine nature" (see 2 Pet. 1:4). Stott was never more helpful or accurate than when he wrote about this two-fold aspect:

> This double duty of a Christian—negative and positive—is the consistent, reiterated teaching of the scripture. Thus we are to deny ourselves *and* to follow Christ. We are to put off what belongs to our old life *and* put on what belongs to our new life. We are to put to death our earthly members *and* set our minds on heavenly things. We are to crucify the flesh *and* to walk in the Spirit. It is the ruthless rejection of the one in combination with the relentless pursuit of the other which scripture enjoins upon us as the secret of holiness. Only so can we hope to be fit for the Master's use.[5]

At this point we can recognize the full course of spiritual events which can lead to the boldness and confidence it takes to think of yourself as gifted . . . to the point you actually begin to exercise your gift for service.

Briefly stated, you consecrate your life by taking both the negative and positive actions which are necessary to purify it. Once your life is consecrated, a sequence of events will be set in motion. You will experience the veritable *power* of God in the transformation of your life that will eventuate in greater assurance of his *love*, then greater faith—and the sound mind to believe the Holy Spirit *can use* a person like you!

If you already have the motivation to serve God and exercise your spiritual gift, skip the rest of this chapter and press on to the next one. However, if you have a Timothy Temperament, let me be more specific with my instructions.

We have mentioned that 2 Timothy sets forth a two-fold duty—to "flee," then to "follow." However, nothing has been said about "how" to do it. Something more can be said about *method*. And I have found it extremely vital to be painstakingly thorough with instructions about the spiritual way of life. *At this point, you will want to keep Paul's other writings in mind, along with this consideration of what he said to Timothy.* Paul does furnish a precise *technique* for this two-fold activity (flee and follow) in the sixth chapter of Romans . . . which I am certain Timothy would have been acquainted with. After all, Timothy had been with Paul about fifteen years when the letter of 2 Timothy was written. And in Romans 6:22, as in 2 Timothy 2:22, Paul is setting forth the same double duty for holiness of life: "Being made free from sin, *and* become servants to God, ye have your fruit unto holiness" (Rom. 6:22). But in Romans, Paul goes deeper to provide instructions as to the "how" of our double duty.

1. How, then, do you "flee" from inner lusts for a consecrated life? You must turn yourself off to the source of lustful desires. *Sin has a common source.* Sin arises out of a selfish, self-willed, self-centered tendency within which corrupts your inner nature. You are born with that tendency: "We started out bad, being born with evil natures" (Eph. 2:3, TLB). You are naturally selfish. And this evil bias (selfishness) is referred to by various names in the Bible. Sometimes it is called the "flesh"; sometimes, the "old man"; and modern translations often refer to it as your "lower nature." Therefore, to turn yourself off to lustful desires, you must turn yourself off to this source from which they originate.

For example, if water overflows your sink, you don't stop it by mopping up the water—*you turn off the faucet.* Correspondingly, to rid yourself of lusts, you turn off the "old nature" (faucet) from which they flow. (Not that you can ever turn off the faucet of your old nature once and for all. It has a faulty handle; it leaks and turns itself back on.)

The Bible teaches that very thing with regard to "lusts." You can die to (turn off) the "old man" or "old nature" (faucet) from which all lust flows: "Put off . . . the old man, which is corrupt according to the deceitful lusts" (Eph. 4:22).

Now, Romans has startling news at this point. Actually, God has already accomplished this for you. That is, your "old nature" (old man) has already been crucified with Christ, "knowing this, that our old man is crucified with him" (Rom. 6:6). This means your "old nature" was crucified, in principle, at Calvary. *But this principle or "potentiality" becomes a "reality" within your daily experience only as you reckon yourself dead to the actual besetting (oft-repeated) sins which the "old nature" is presently spawning in your life. You actually begin to seek deliverance from your habitual sins . . . one at a time.*

You must die to (turn off) the "old man" (faucet) of sin, and you do so by a *reckoning process*. That is, after recognizing an habitual sin in your life, you claim (by faith) the fact that you are dead to the "old nature" that spawned it—thus dead to the sin: "Likewise *reckon* ye also yourselves to be dead indeed unto sin, but alive unto God through Jesus Christ our Lord" (Rom. 6:11, italics added).

Now "reckon" is a faith word. To "reckon" is to "rely on." You reckon it is so just because God says so. *You bow your head in prayer and tell God that you reckon or rely on the fact that you are dead to some illegitimate desire—just because the Bible says you are!* You exercise an audacious faith to believe you will be unresponsive to that sin today just because of your trust in his Word.

But let me add a few words of caution right here:

(1) When Romans 6 sets forth this instruction, it stresses obedience *from the heart:* "But ye have obeyed from the heart" (Rom. 6:17). This requires, at the least, that you exercise your willpower to cooperate with all you have asked God to do for you. For example, if you are exercising faith to reckon yourself dead to a sin of gossip, then your part would be to stop listening to the same. In the case of a gambling habit, you would do your part by staying away from gambling establishments. If a student is reckoning himself dead to the temptation to cheat in school, his part would be to study so that cheating becomes less necessary (and stop taking cheat notes into class).

Although your effort would be ineffective in itself, God adds his effort to yours and honors your faith by setting you free from habitual sins. But God will not strengthen your moral fiber *apart* from your cooperative effort, weak as it might be. So be certain you have done your part and "resisted unto blood, striving against sin" (Heb. 12:4).

(2) Secondly, God also demands that you *ask for* that added strength the Holy Spirit will supply. After all, the Holy Spirit does provide the power to carry out the execution: "If ye *through the Spirit* do mortify [put to death] the deeds of the body, ye shall live" (Rom. 8:13, italics added). And your faith is expressed in the asking!

How, then, do you get set free from evil desires in order to consecrate your life? Let us suppose, for instance, that you have a gluttony problem. You lust for food. Simply bow your head at the beginning of each day (repeat throughout the day as necessary) and pray something like this: "Lord, I believe I will be dead to gluttony today because you say I am—in the Scriptures. I do *reckon* myself dead to the sin of gluttony. I will exercise my own willpower to resist it, in cooperation with your help (I will diet and stay clear of overly-enticing eating places) . . . and I trust the Holy Spirit to carry out the execution."

What is the way to purify your life? Negatively, you seek out your besetting sin and die.

2. Now let us turn from the negative to the positive side of a purified life. How, then, do you *follow* after righteousness. You follow after righteousness by a *yielding process:* "Neither yield ye your members as instruments of unrighteousness unto sin: but yield yourselves unto God, as those that are alive from the dead, and your members as instruments of righteousness unto God" (Rom. 6:13).

The second step toward a purified life is to *yield* your life as an instrument of righteousness unto God. Furthermore, the verse above indicates precisely how this is done.

(1) According to Romans 6:13, you actually yield the "members" of your body: eyes, ears, mind, lips, feet, and so forth, for God's use. Yielding is a practical, active matter. Paul is not speaking merely of a state of mind here. He is saying you actually place your members— your hands, lips, feet, etc.—at God's disposal for righteous use (God's use). For instance, at the slightest impression that God would like to say something through your lips, you practice instant obedience and say it.

(2) Furthermore, according to Romans 6:13, you yield the members of your body as *instruments*. An instrument is a tool which is used

for a specific task. Paul is focusing down to a fine point. You are to yield your members as *tools* for *specific* tasks . . . as God impresses you throughout the day,

Furthermore, Paul was highly selective in his choice of the word *yield*. To yield requires action, yes, but *dependent action* (as over against independent action). That is, when you yield, you place yourself in the hands of another for his use of you. You place yourself at his disposal, counting on his strength. This verse is speaking of yielding yourself as an instrument in the hands of an all-powerful God. The word for "yield" is translated here from the original Greek word *paristano*, which carries with it the connotation of "placing alongside." You act in cooperation with another, exerting yourself . . . *but in dependence upon his power.*

To sum up what Romans 6:13 is saying: you are to instantly yield the members of your body as tools for the specific tasks you feel impressed that God would have you do in the course of each given day . . . and take action in dependence upon his power. Again, Paul is not merely speaking of a vague, conjured mental activity, but of a life-style of action in which you practice instant obedience to specific tasks.

For example, if in the course of your daily round of activities, you feel impressed of God to give a hand to someone in need, you extend that hand and depend upon God for the strength to accomplish the task. If you feel impressed of God to visit someone in the hospital, your feet turn in that direction and you depend upon God to fill your lips with the right words to say.

So, this book is not only a call to noble service. We must also sound the call to a *consecrated* life, which is the one great prerequisite for Christian service in general and spiritual gifts in particular. I assure you! The biblical techniques of consecration suggested here have been hammered out on the anvil of experience. They can be trusted. They are tried and true—they represent God's way. No man or woman ever lived through whom God has not done something of grand spiritual significance when they cared enough to ruthlessly reject the sin in their life on the one hand, in combination with the relentless pursuit of righteousness on the other! But this is accomplished only in dependence upon God by "reckoning" in the first instance and by "yielding" in the latter.

So I lift this trumpet to my lips and sound the call to service. Let those that follow come forth to die . . . for on the other side of your death to sin will be a resurrection to righteousness, which will merit you a sure place of honor among the servants of your King. (These instructions ought to be sufficient for the spiritual preparation which is necessary to serve God effectively. But I have written an entire book which discusses spiritual fullness in considerably more detail . . . and such a book will be a much needed preparation for some).[6]

The only sure remedy for a Timothy Temperament is to "stir up the gift which is in you." To get right down to where we live, few Christians will ever effectively exercise a spiritual gift apart from a *consecrated* life through which timidity is knocked out of them by a head-on collision with the Holy Spirit. A consecrated life is inevitably transfigurating (Rom. 12:2). It will trigger Paul's cycle, as we have mentioned with regard to 2 Timothy 2:22: the Holy Spirit will *transform* you with God's power, which *transmits* to you God's love, which *transfuses* you with the faith of mind to trust God in the exercise of your gift (in that order)!

It is unthinkable, from the standpoint of God's grace, that so many of us are spiritually impoverished with regard to Christian service. A lukewarm spiritual experience has never been palatable to God (Rev. 3:16). Let me ask you, "Would God have invested someone as precious as Christ to procure a stagnate, useless Christian experience?" I think not!

Yet, God is reaping such poor return from the investment of his Son. He must respond to us much like the great old king who had a favorite lord in his kingdom. The winsome lord was a nobleman of perfection, greatly honored by his king and revered among the people.

One day a runaway chariot came crashing through the palace city. To everyone's horror, a little boy was playing too far out in the street. It seemed inevitable the little fellow would be trampled by the horses' hooves. But the king's trusted lord was standing nearby. In the flash of a moment, he dove at the boy, knocking him out of the way. But the trampling hooves of the horses and the iron wheels of the chariot smashed across his body, leaving it crushed like putty, lying there lifeless in the street.

The old king was thrown into deep remorse over the death of his lord. He asked to see the fellow that his nobleman had died to save. And when they brought the dirty, unkempt, unclaimed street urchin in before him, the king exclaimed, "Oh! Is this all I get in return for my lord?"

What has God in you?

Notes

1. Handley C. G. Moule, *The Second Epistle to Timothy* (The Devotional Commentary series, Religious Tract Society, 1905), p. 18.

2. John R. W. Stott, *Guard the Gospel* (Downers Grove, Illinois: Inter-Varsity Press, 1973), p. 30.

3. *Ibid.*, p. 20.

4. Bruce Larson and Ralph Osborne, *The Emerging Church* (Waco, Texas: Word Books, 1970), p. 68.

5. Stott, p. 75.

6. James Mahoney, *Journey into Fullness* (Nashville: Broadman Press, 1974).

4

Route #1

God's will for your life will be most fully experienced as you press on to the particular type of service in which you are spiritually gifted (supernaturally motivated and enabled). *This is Route #1 into God's will for your life.* Let's temporarily confine our investigation to the discovery of your spiritual gift, for the Scriptures clearly teach us to be enlightened about this subject: "Now concerning spiritual gifts, brethren, I would not have you ignorant" (1 Cor. 12:1).

What are spiritual gifts? Surely, no question is asked more frequently by those deeply interested in ministry.

To begin with, let me formulate a definitive statement: *A spiritual gift is a supernatural endowment of motivation and ability for effective Christian service.* Examine this definition. You will notice, basically, a spiritual gift is for *service.* Indeed, a spiritual gift could be referred to as your "service gift." Furthermore, the definition suggests three basic characteristics of a gift. And to understand what a spiritual gift is, we must further define each of these key aspects. A spiritual gift is: (1) A *supernatural endowment:* that which happens beyond natural laws and understanding, that which is beyond human ability to execute or explain. (2) A *motivation:* an inner desire to serve God in a certain way. (3) An *ability:* a special enabling to serve, which originates from the Holy Spirit.

With these three factors in mind, let me elaborate on this definition for a still more thorough understanding.

Spiritual Gifts Are Transcendent to You

A Spiritual Gift is a "supernatural endowment." It is a divine act of *supernatural* power, energized by the Holy Spirit. To exercise your gift is to serve in a power beyond yourself, *transcendent* to your own abilities.

It has been my privilege to lead several conference groups on a "Journey into Usefulness." In these conferences, we have sought to discover our spiritual gifts. And those who followed through and began exercising their gift in the Spirit's power began to count for God with telling effect. The following are their random remarks, written later, about what it meant to serve in power:

"Effective service has added a remarkable sense of inward satisfaction to my life."

"Discovering my area of service . . . and the resultant blessings of God upon my service have added a deeper sense of *purpose* to my life. My life has become significant."

"An unsuspected benefit of exercising my gift has been the development of deep and abiding friendship with those God has used me to help."

"My initial experiences of successful service were self-motivating . . . urging me on to further, greater tasks."

"Hallelujah, to be used of God has released springs of joy in my soul."

"Power, sheer power, as I have witnessed God use me to bring healing and transformation of life . . . and a consciousness of others has replaced a 'hypersensitive self-consciousness' which had plagued my mind with doubts and anxieties."

"I have discovered the more I am used of God in the exercise of my gift of mercy, the more my own life is shaped and changed into the likeness of my Lord."

All these remarks reveal a diversity of blessings. However, there were several other results which everyone seemed to experience in common. All who exercised a gift in the Spirit's power shared the following effects: to be consistently used of God will *deepen your assurance of his favor, enlarge your faith, broaden your concern, intensify your zeal, make you an inevitable blessing to others, and enlarge your understanding of God's will for your life.*

However, void of such an experience, those of little faith tend to openly discredit any claim of supernatural power for service. The long lines of people in America who crowded to see the motion picture *The Exorcist* only testify of a curiosity with the baser aspects of spiritual phenomena—they certainly did not testify of national acceptance of benevolent spiritual power.

Indeed, uplifting, supernatural, and miraculous spiritual activity are held suspect in our time. For example, my family resided in a rather small town. When not traveling, we immensely enjoyed our life there. Once a couple came through the town for a one-day teaching conference, which was held in a local theater but was sponsored by a church group. At the close of the conference, those interested were encouraged to remain for a special prayer and healing service. *The couple felt led to exercise a spiritual gift of mercy by praying for the sick.*

It caused quite a response. Some people promptly excused themselves. Most remained. However, many who stayed were ever so skeptical. The after-service was not without some rather spectacular experiences. A friend of ours was one of those who experienced a healing. She is a bright, spiritual young lady. She is well-educated, sophisticated, and wealthy, the sort of person that would shy away from exhibitionism and sensationalism. She walked forward in quiet faith; a prayer was offered, and she experienced a healing. Several months after the meeting, I spoke personally with another lady who was miraculously healed. The pastor of my church went forward, a prayer was offered on his behalf, and he said, "The next moment the power of God struck me with such force I would have been lying flat on my back if someone had not caught me from behind." Here is a well-educated, dedicated, established minister of a church which is affiliated with one of America's largest Protestant denominations, and he is telling of having been, as he called it, "slain in the Spirit"!

But the most interesting thing to me was the reaction of people in our town. The service did not go unnoticed. There were not too many who responded with a casual remark like, "Well, God has blessed with some more wonderful healings."

To the contrary, many people responded with verbal disbelief. Many expressed themselves antagonistically. Two ministers felt urged upon to denounce the meeting from their pulpits. Many who were sympathetic were nevertheless surprised. I am not taking issue with anyone about this specific incident, so much as I am calling attention to one thing: The frame of mind in the community revealed general doubt about actual demonstrations of the supernatural power of God. And I suspect this reflects the prevailing attitude in America.

Indeed, it might well take a supernatural revelation to get us to believe in miraculous human experience. One reason I wanted to write this book was to "stand in the middle of the floor" and declare my belief in the reality of supernatural experience within the spiritual way of life. If this classifies me with a fraternity of spiritual "oddfellows," so be it! Just realize that any agreement on your part might constitute your inclusion in it with me. Our generation of Christians does not think in terms of supernatural possibilities. Francis Schaeffer warns that you can be so infiltrated by twentieth-century thinking, you can live most of your life as if the supernatural were not there: "Our generation is overwhelmingly naturalistic. There is an almost complete commitment to the concept of the uniformity of natural causes in a closed system. This is a distinguishing mark of our age." [1]

There seems to be almost complete agreement that man has jettisoned his supernatural canopy and has come "down to earth" in his belief in a naturalistic world. Peter L. Berger begins one of his books with the statement:

> If commentators on the contemporary situation of religion agree about anything, it is that the supernatural has departed from the modern world. This departure may be stated in such dramatic formulations as God is dead or the post-Christian era, or it may be undramatically assumed as a global and probably irreversible trend. [2]

The Hartford sociologist Pitirim Sorokin labeled ours as the *sensate* generation. Sensate means "empirical, this worldly, secular, humanistic, pragmatic, utilitarian, contractural, epicurean or hedonistic and the like." [3]

Nevertheless, I agree with Francis Schaeffer who says that naturalism (which excludes supernatural experience) is the greatest single reason for the loss of reality in Christian lives. That is why so many Christians are spiritually dull, if not dead. "Being a biblical Christian means living in the supernatural now, not only theoretically, but in practice." [4] Tell me, how long has it been since you have believed God for a miracle in your life? How long has it been since you have seen things happen in your life which take God to explain?

However, we must be equally careful not to equate the *supernatural* with the *sensational*. One of the most powerful demonstrations of a spiritual gift I have ever witnessed was a little lady who exercised her gift of mercy by tirelessly maintaining endless rounds of quiet, weekly visitation in old-folks homes. There was nothing spectacular about it. However, only God could have motivated her rigid schedule. And for the few of us who witnessed the glowing countenances of the bedfast to whom she ministered, there was the evident smack of the divine in the "*Son*shine" she brought into their lives.

A second aspect should be emphasized.

Spiritual Gifts Are Triggered Within You

There is also a sense in which a spiritual gift is a *motivation*. It is a compulsive inner motivation for service. It is a kind of "triggering" action within, by which God stimulates you to serve. It is the means by which God works "in you to know and do his will" (Phil. 2:13) with regard to service.

Think for a moment. In what way is a spiritual gift divine (divinely initiated)? That is, in what way is your gift the effort of God within your life? In what manner are you enabled, by your gift, to serve in a power beyond natural ability? How can you distinguish your gift as a God-wrought activity?

Again, it is a matter of motivation. You are gifted in that you are motivated to serve in a certain way. For example, a person with the gift of teaching will study because of an insatiable thirst for knowledge. His thirst for knowledge will be exceeded only by his desire to share what he has learned. But the same could be said of the gift of prophecy. The prophet speaks because he has to. He has a word from God which inwardly inflames, and the message demands release like steam from a teakettle. God reveals a message so vividly that the prophet has a compulsion to proclaim it. The message itself fills him with desire. His gift is recognized by his compulsion to speak forth. As Paul once exclaimed, "Necessity is laid upon me; yea, woe unto me if I preach not the gospel" (1 Cor. 9:16). Other men may hold their peace. But those exercising the gift of prophecy will be inwardly compelled to speak forth. An overwhelming compulsion moves a teacher to instruct or a prophet to speak, and it is at just that point you can say he is supernaturally empowered since the initiative comes from God. And this divine initiative helps to mark his effort as a spiritual gift. It is in this motivation and the effect of his service that you can say one is energized beyond himself and his own abilities. This takes God to explain!

Moreover, each gift has its own specific kind of motivation which we will discuss later. But it is sufficient for the moment to see that spiritual gifts are Spirit-initiated motivations for service.

Finally, spiritual gifts are transcendent to you, triggered within you, and transmitted through you.

Spiritual Gifts Are Transmitted Through You

You see, there is a sense in which a spiritual gift is not *something you receive* so much as it is an *ability to be used.* Your gift is not something in itself which you get from God to use as you choose. It is an ability to be used of God in areas of special enablement.

Spiritual gifts are an enabling for service. What you actually receive is the privilege of knowing you can be mightily used along a certain route of service and the motivation to do so. Spiritual gifts refer to the activity the Holy Spirit executes through your life. The Scriptures refer to them as "the manifestation of the Spirit" (1 Cor. 12:7). So you are gifted in that there is a definite route of service along which God will especially work through your life to accomplish his redemptive purpose in this world. That is Route #1 for your life. You should major in that area of service, and your gift is the fact that the Holy Spirit motivates you and will empower your efforts along that line of service.

In defining spiritual gifts, many stress the point that gifts are *not* natural talents. "We have missed the teaching of the scriptures if we think that 'spiritual gifts' refer to using natural talents for the glory of God." [5]

Perhaps this distinction is justified. Christians often say a person is "gifted," with reference to their native talents. For instance, we refer to a person's outstanding singing ability as his "gift." But a *natural gift* is not necessarily the same as a *spiritual gift.* Therefore, some have stressed that any natural human ability which you were "born with" cannot be your spiritual gift, for your spiritual gift is received through the regenerative spiritual experience of becoming a Christian (your *second* birth). The Holy Spirit imparts your spiritual gift upon his entrance into your life at the point of your Christian conversion.

On the other hand, we can make too much of this distinction between your talent and your gift. Certainly, to differentiate between a "natural gift" and a "spiritual gift" is *not* to say that one is given apart from any consideration of the other. I believe Ralph Neighbour came closer to the truth of it when he said:

> But while it is true that the gift . . . is not merely a natural endowment, it is also perfectly certain that the Spirit of God never bestows a spiritual gift for service except upon men who have natural endowments that will enable them to use it. There is nothing in the economy of God out of joint and out of place . . . the gift will be bestowed upon men who have natural aptitudes and fitness and endowments for their work.[6]

Furthermore, while your gift will not *necessarily* be commensurate with your talent, it *can* be! That is, the Holy Spirit might enlarge your talent by infusing his energies and abilities. Suddenly an old talent might take on new significance, be carried out with a newfound effortlessness, and result in multiplied effectiveness. This is more consistent with what the Scriptures *actually* teach will happen to us at conversion. For instance, 2 Corinthians records the following statement which describes a conversion experience: "Therefore if any man be in Christ, he is a new creature: old things are passed away; behold, all things are become new" (2 Cor. 5:17). But take another look at that last phrase, for the verse can better be translated: "Therefore if any man be in Christ, he is a new creature: old things are passed away; behold, [old] things are become new."

You become a new creature at conversion in the sense that your relationship to things is changed. You begin to see and experience things from a new perspective. *Old things pass away* in terms of their former significance to your life. And those same *old things become new* in

terms of your new relationship to them. For example, sexual desire
can pass away as lust but return as expression of love and responsible
sex within marriage. Your keen power of observation passes away as
a critical nature and returns as discernment. The inner drive to attain
can pass away as vain ambition but return as commitment to the cause
of Christ. Money and material things can pass away as ends in themselves
but return as means to greater ends. Yes, and ability can pass away
as a *natural talent* and return as a *service gift* . . . when quickened
by the Spirit!

Let us repeat: a spiritual gift is "the manifestation of the Spirit"
(1 Cor. 12:7). Your gift is what the Spirit accomplishes through you
for others to be blessed.

Now let me review what I have said in another sentence form:

A spiritual gift is: (1) transcendent to you (as a supernatural endowment); (2) triggered within you (as a motivation); and (3) transmitted
through you (as an ability to be used)—for effective Christian service.

To watch just one commercial jet roar off into the skies is to realize
the need for a more explosive and forceful Christian witness in our
atomic age. We need an empowering for Christian service. And God
has promised just that . . . at least one area of service in which he
will use each and every Christian in a most powerful way. Just remember: to exercise your spiritual gift means God is at work. You
are just as sufficient as the boundless resources of God, for service gifts
are *transcendent* to you, but *triggered within you,* and *transmitted
through you* as a manifestation of God's Holy Spirit. They represent
God's finest effort with your life . . . to do something about the needs
of this world, today!

Notes

1. Francis A. Schaeffer, *True Spirituality* (Wheaton, Illinois: Tyndale House Publishers, 1971), p. 60.

2. Peter L. Berger, *A Rumor of Angels* (Garden City, New York: Doubleday & Company, 170), p. 1.

3. Herman Kahn and Anthony J. Wierner, *The Year 2000—A Framework for Speculation on the Next Thirty-Three Years* (New York: Macmillan Co., 1967), p. 7.

4. Schaeffer, pp. 60-64.

5. G. Campbell Morgan, *Evangelism* (Westwood, N.J.: Fleming H. Revell Co., 1964), p. 47.

6. Ralph W. Neighbor, Jr., *This Gift Is Mine* (Nashville: Broadman Press, 1974), p. 22.

5
Right on . . . to Your Gift

The surfers use an expression, "right on," to describe the perfect ride on a perfect wave. You must catch the wave just right—then it will take you where you want to go.

Just so, there is a biblical account of those who caught onto God's will for *their* lives . . . and if you get caught up in their experience, it will take you "right on" into God's will for your service in general and your spiritual gift in particular.

In Acts 3—4 we have the first record of Christian service after Pentecost, and it provides tremendous insight into how the original apostles discovered God's will for their lives, *in terms of service*. Let's see how they did it. The passage captures them in the course of exercising their service gift of prophecy, and they set the example.

Acts 3—4 are fertile passages of Scripture. Most significantly, they clearly reveal the fundamental dynamic of *spiritual gifts*, for the prime ingredient of a spiritual gift is motivation. The most vital, intrinsic quality of a spiritual gift is the inner compulsion to serve God, and to serve in a particular way. This compelling incentive for service is what distinguishes your gift as the effort of God in your life.

In the case of Peter and John, they were impelled to act as God's spokesmen or prophets. *A cursory analysis will reveal five vital stages with regard to their motivation for service.* How, then, do you discover God's will for your service? Look for these five factors of spiritual motivation:

Factor #1: Divine Inception

One of the most obvious factors with regard to the motivation of Peter and John was the *source* of their compulsion to serve. Their motivation for service was one of divine inception: "Now when they saw the boldness of Peter and John, and perceived that they were unlearned and ignorant men, they marvelled; and they took knowledge of them, *that they had been with Jesus*" (Acts 4:13, italics added). The bold ministry of Peter and John was such that observers assumed "they had been with Jesus."

But I have asked myself, *Where had they been with Jesus?* The fact is they had been many places with Jesus. To which place is our Scripture verse referring? Peter and John had been with Jesus when he fed the 5,000 beside the Sea of Galilee. They had been with Jesus when he delivered his great Sermon on the Mount. They had been with Jesus when he healed the sick. They were present on the day of his glorious transfiguration. They had been with Jesus all along, and they were with him in the end. They were present in the upper room, and they followed him to Calvary.

However, as marvelous as these times were, *none* of these experiences propelled them into their tremendous ministry as extolled in the book of Acts. Where had they been with Jesus, then, which could have accounted for their bold ministry? What really motivated Peter and John was that *they had been with Jesus after his resurrection, and experienced the power of that resurrection at Pentecost!*

After the crucifixion of Christ, the disciples were just about ready to throw in the towel. They were doubtful, disappointed, and despondent. In fear of persecution, they were meeting secretly, behind locked doors, when Christ suddenly appeared in their midst (John 20:19). Christ revealed himself to them; they realized he was alive; and the result was transforming. Christ is alive! That is the message they burst forth to proclaim. Having discovered that, they simply *had to* share it!

In the same manner, *you can know Jesus well, just as did the disciples, without having fully experienced the power of his resurrection.* This is what Paul has reference to when he shares the goal of his life: "That I may know him, *and* the power of his resurrection" (Phil. 3:10, italics added).

Now see this same verse as rendered in *The Amplified Bible:* "[For my determined purpose is] that I may know Him—that I may progressively become more deeply and intimately acquainted with Him. . . . and that I may in the same way come to know the power outflowing from His resurrection [which it exerts over believers] " (Phil. 3:10).

You see, something happens to you when you have been with Christ enough to experience his resurrection power. Oh, to be sure, you *cannot* be present on the day of Christ's resurrection like the first disciples were. Nevertheless, you can experience the very same resurrection power the disciples did at Pentecost. Simply allow him to *fully* come alive in your life. I am not referring to your salvation experience, although that is when Christ comes to indwell. Rather, *I am referring to the time when Christ, having entered, begins to gain real control of your life, enough to command your life for his cause.*

The most accomplished and consistent Christian laymen of my acquaintance attribute their motivation for service to a time when Christ began to renew them into such newness of life that it was, indeed, like experiencing the same resurrection power which brought Christ up from the grave. I have heard layman after layman say the same thing. Having experienced renewed life, they are moved to great deeds of service. You can always take knowledge of such men—they will have been with Jesus and will have experienced his resurrection power. Their service is of divine inception.

Paul speaks of this power to change our lives: "But if the Spirit of him that raised up Jesus from the dead dwell in you, he that raised up Christ from the dead shall also quicken your mortal bodies by his Spirit that dwelleth in you" (Rom. 8:11).

I think of one of the most exciting laymen I have ever known. He was serving God spasmodically when I first came to know him. But I recall the day he came to Christ with an insurmountable need through which Christ came fully and powerfully alive in him. He never got over it. For the first time since the early days of his conversion, he had really experienced the power of God in his life. He was never the same after that. His life since then has centered on service that Christ might come alive in others.

The question is, "Have you ever stood with Jesus before an open tomb into which he has discarded the graveclothes of your old life and then experienced the pulsating wonder of new life—*to the point that you want God to use you for others?*" When you actually experience the power of the resurrected Christ within, setting you free from the bondage of your old way of life, then you will be able to believe he has the power to make you an effective servant—and you will be compelled to serve.

The question then naturally follows, "How do you appropriate this resurrection power?" And the answer to that question is: you appropriate this resurrection power *by the consecration of your life!*

As discussed in chapter 3, the very steps set forth in Romans which are necessary for the consecration of your life are the same steps by which you experience Christ's resurrection power:

> Reckoning: "Likewise reckon ye also yourselves *to be dead unto sin, but alive unto God* through Jesus Christ our Lord" (Rom. 6:11, italics mine).

> Yielding: "Yield yourselves unto God, *as those that are alive from the dead,* and your members as instruments of righteousness unto God" (Rom. 6:13, italics mine).

(Note the wording of each verse, how Paul describes each activity in terms of a resurrection.)

If you wish to know how to carry out these verses, simply review the instructions at the end of chapter 3.

Romans 6 also teaches that this experience will eventuate in service: "Being made free from sin, *and become servants to God,* ye have your fruit" (Rom. 6:22, italics added).

The motivation for Christian service is of *divine inception.* It comes when you have consecrated (set apart) your life to Jesus and experienced his resurrection power, setting you free from bondage to your old way of life and quickening you to a new life of service for him.

Factor #2: Intense Compulsion

The decisive factor in motivating you to serve has to do with the *intensity* of your motivation. There is a velocity factor in motivation. It all depends on the intensity of your desire to serve. Be assured you will never adequately exercise an effective ministry or a spiritual gift until you arrive at a point where you just *have to* serve him. Love, like water, has a boiling point. And when that point is reached, there is explosive power to propel and compel. Remember, Peter and John were God's spokesmen. Yet, the authorities had actually "commanded them not to speak at all nor teach in the name of Jesus" (Acts 4:18). But Peter and John could not cease speaking, even under the threat of imprisonment: "For we cannot but speak the things which we have seen and heard" (v. 20, italics added). They simply *had to* share their message.

The compulsion to serve was so intense for Peter and John that they did so even under threat of punishment. Just so, most Christians will never exercise a spiritual gift apart from such an *intense* compulsion to serve that they will do so at any cost. None of us are likely to exercise our gift apart from such motivation. In the first place, such sacrificial service goes against the grain of a carnal (self-centered) Christian life-style. Furthermore, we all have our "hang-ups," not the least of which will be the common malady called *fear*.

Just as *timidity* is the one great harbinger mitigating against a serious consideration of our gift, *fear* prevents us from the action we must take to discover it. You see, the devil has done his work on most of us. For one thing, he has woven harsh treatment, lovelessness, and intimidation through the length and breadth of society, so that many of us grow up with a large number of suppressed fears within us. When these fears begin to collect, they form "fear complexes" or phobias which lurk like labyrinthian monsters in the depths of our subconscious minds. These phobias fling off stimuli, like fiery darts, into our nervous systems each time we are intimidated and every time we face the unknown.

Such fears are a great deterrent. They hinder Christian service in general and the exercise of a spiritual gift in particular.

Even the bold and mighty Jeremiah at first balked at his special calling. Although God had ordained him to serve as a prophet, he was quite unwilling and vigorously protested, "Ah, Lord God! behold, I cannot speak" (Jer. 1:6).

You see, Jeremiah was *"afraid* of their faces" (Jer. 1:8). Satan's fiery darts had found their mark. Jeremiah was struck with fear.

Most of us are far too insecure to serve God or exercise some spiritual gift. We are fearful of failure and ridicule. We are fearful of the untried. And we are fearful of change! Therefore, it takes an *intense compulsion* for some of us to "risk it" in Christian service. Without really realizing it, we are too fearful unless we *have to*. But let's pause for a *deeper* look at human motivation in order to understand how God's resurrection power can produce the compelling energy necessary for service.

Someone has pointed out that the church has mistakenly used the "suction" method to carry out her mission . . . trying to draw all the outsiders into our sanctuary. What we should be using is an "explosive" method, exploding into the world to serve as witnesses of him. And, I might add, our explosive propulsion into Christian service, like an atomic bomb, will take the form of a chain reaction. As we previously stated, the cycle goes from *power* to *love* to *sound mind* to *service!*

Let me elaborate. When Christ comes alive in you with such resurrection *power* that your life is transformed for the better, you will develop a greater assurance of God's *perfect (full) love* for you (1 John 2:5). And when you become more assured of his loving care, you will find the *faith of mind* to fully trust God, enough to do what he wants you to do . . . *in service*. Do you see it? *Power* produces a response of *love*, which results in a *mind* to *serve*.

Now let's *apply this cycle to our fear problem* . . . as it relates to Christian service.

(1) Experiencing God's power in your life assures you of his perfect (full) love for you.

(2) Then, as the Scriptures state, *"perfect love casteth out fear"* (1 John 4:18, italics added).

(3) However, it is to be noted that perfect love casts out fear by producing the kind of faith that expels it.

By the way, this cycle provides us with an interesting insight. That is, that the opposite of faith is not doubt. The opposite of *faith* is *fear!* Jesus indicated this: "Why are ye fearful, O ye of little faith" (Matt. 8:26). Think on it. You can have some faith mixed with a little doubt. "I believe, help thou my unbelief" (Mark 9:24). But *fear is doubt inflamed!* And while doubt may cause you to hesitate, fear incapacitates.

Fear and faith are opposites, but faith can excel. In the book of Numbers, the children of Israel are exhorted to put away their fear and go on in to conquer the Promised Land. ". . . The Lord is with us, fear them not" (Num. 14:9). But they failed to do so because they

were too afraid. And the New Testament commentary on this failure
reveals they were *fearful* because of their *unbelief* (Heb. 3:19). Fear
and faith are opposites. So, the antidote to fear is an all-encompassing
faith. The shield of faith can quench the fiery darts of fear (Eph. 6:16).

For example, some members of the Richard Hogue evangelistic team
were talking with one another as they stood on a hillside. While they
were conversing, Richard's young son, Israel, was playing down a steep
embankment. Israel was only three years old, and someone commented,
"He certainly is *fearless* to play down there so far away." Then a second
team member remarked, "Yes, he is unafraid because he knows his
daddy is right here to help him."

Precisely! Young Israel had never run down that hill before, so his
faith didn't arise out of confidence in the situation. It was the strength
of his father's love for him that made him bold. Yes, perfect (mature)
love produces a faith which, in turn, expels fear, just as electricity
produces a light that expels darkness!

Yes, God wants to come alive in your life in such a way as to set
off a chain reaction which will explode you right through such barriers
as fear, thrusting you into this world to serve as a witness of him.
Without fully understanding it, you will find yourself moved by an
intense compulsion to serve.

There is a sense in which we ought to serve God out of sheer
obedience, whether we feel motivated or not. But we will never minister
adequately until our love for Christ reaches a boiling point and we
simply *have to* serve him. If you have tapped into God's resurrection
power for your life to the point you have an "intense compulsion"
to serve, then you are ready for our next principle—that of *rational
selection*.

Factor #3: Rational Selection

It is significant to note that Peter and John were motivated along
one particular line of service—they were moved to *speak* (prophesy)
about what they had learned from God. "For we cannot but speak"
(Acts 4:20). After they were really "turned on," they made a very natural
and rational selection as to what they were to do.

The point is—when you reach the place where you just *have to* serve Christ, *see what it is you most want to do precisely at that moment . . . in terms of the seven areas of service set forth in Romans 12.* That will be your gift! In other words, the desire of that moment will indicate the area of service in which you are spiritually gifted.

But this is *not* to imply that everyone who has experienced a great desire to serve Christ will have discovered the area in which he is gifted.

Some do not know to look. They have never been taught they have a spiritual gift.

Some misinterpret what they see. They mistake natural abilities for a spiritual gift.

Some do not want what they see. They fail to recognize the value of their gift because it demands they work "behind the scenes"—it is unspectacular.

Consequently, some have been moved to serve God along certain lines but failed to follow through into faithfulness. Others have begun serving, then quit.

Nevertheless, thank God, others have come away from high times of life-changing inspiration with a desire to serve God in a particular area of ministry, only to recognize their gift and exercise it as men after God's own heart!

Factor #4: Decisive Acceptance

Your spiritual gift is yours at the moment of your Christian conversion. For the Holy Spirit enters immediately—to supernaturally enable you to serve in a certain way. However, the "gift of service can remain latent, awaiting discovery and utilization.

So you will never effectively exercise a spiritual gift apart from a time of *decisive acceptance,* when you acknowledge your spiritual gift as your basic responsibility of service. And decisive acceptance means a *conscious, definite, lasting decision to exercise your gift, no matter what.* You cross the line of no return and sell out in your commitment. You will find the decisive nature of their commitment was a distinguishing feature in the manner in which Peter and John exercised their gift of prophecy. Peter and John had decisively accepted their call to speak for God as a heavenly mandate for which they would sooner die than deny.

Consider their circumstances. They had been thrown into a dingy, foul-smelling dungeon. They were twice threatened by the authorities, told to speak no more, and escaped severe punishment only because public sentiment happened to be with them at the time (Acts 4:17-18,21).

But they were not to be silenced. They resisted the authorities to their faces (v. 20). Then they called a prayer meeting to pray for even more boldness of speech (v. 29). And they fearlessly continued their ministry: "And with great power gave the apostles witness of the resurrection of the Lord Jesus" (v. 33). These first disciples were irrevocably committed to the exercise of their gift. The fiber of their commitment was tough enough to last. It stood the test of troubled times.

But *your* decision to exercise a spiritual gift must be like theirs—a decisive commitment. Your gift will never be developed by a half-hearted, uncertain effort.

It will never be easy to faithfully serve God or exercise a spiritual gift. God will expect so much of your life that you will want to quit ten times over before your ministry becomes a polished, magnificent force for God in this world. Oh, this is not to say that everything will be expected of you initially. But the very first activities of service will be met with opposition (as God allows it). And you will experience those times when your difficulties will accelerate into crisis proportions.

Mark these words. *There is that within the nature of Christian service which demands a depth of commitment equaled by few other endeavors in life.* Trouble and trial are "within the very nature of Christian service" because Christ's cause runs contrary to the course of our world system. As mentioned previously, the way of ungodliness is a *broad road* through a *wide gate—with heavy traffic.* To the contrary, the way of godliness is depicted as a *narrow path* through a *straight gate—*and is *comparatively untraveled* (Matt. 7:13-14).

The heavier traffic is on the broad road because it leads downhill—it is most easily traveled, *but the narrow pathway leads right back up through the middle of the broad road in the opposite direction.* It is uphill and counter-flowing, against the current of the times. No one will just "drift" into effective Christian service. It is hard-going, uphill all the way. But it leads ever higher to plateaus of ever-ascending glory. It is the only trip worth taking.

But that is exactly the point, isn't it! Serving God *is* worth the trouble. And when geared to redemptive action, your service gift represents your primary obedience to an appreciative God, your greatest opportunity of service to mankind, and it is an irreplaceable ingredient for the total fulfillment of your life. God has granted this gift to provide *purpose* for your existence in this world, a purpose which is enormously significant and eternally self-fulfilling. Who in the whole, wide world is more important than a man on mission for God? Eternity will certainly place this in perspective!

But the discovery and development of your spiritual gift waits upon your *decisive acceptance*. God has based the discovery of your service-gift on what I call the "Sell-out Principle."

Jesus told of a pearl merchant who discovered a "pearl of great price," *and sold all his other pearls to purchase that one* (Matt. 13:45-46). That parable presents a principle which is applicable to the discovery of spiritual gifts—in that you will never likely discover your service gift until you come to the realization of its worth. You must recognize it as an enabling of such value it would almost be worth trading all your other talents and attributes for. Your gift is a pearl of great price. You must give it priority over all natural talents and human abilities. You must pay the price to develop it. The Bible teaches that you are to "earnestly desire and zealously cultivate" your gift (1 Cor. 12:31, Amplified).

A "decisive acceptance," then, requires your understanding of the worth of a gift. God will not cast his pearl among swine, that is, *to one who lacks the capacity to appreciate it* (Matt. 7:6). A decisive acceptance should be a definite, responsible act. Did not our Lord teach us to "count the cost" before accepting a particular task? And Jesus went on to explain this as a willingness to "forsake all," if necessary, in the fulfillment of that task (Luke 14:28). A decisive acceptance should be an irrevocable one. Receive your enabling for service appreciatively, and head out to serve—*never looking back*. For Jesus said, "No man, having put his hand to the plough, and looking back, is fit for the kingdom of God" (Luke 9:62).

But such an acceptance of your spiritual ministry will be appreciably strengthened by the next factor.

Factor #5: Sustaining Verification

God will verify a spiritual ministry with supernatural results. These results will have a two-fold effect. They will *sustain* your desire to serve and will also *verify* your efforts as the work of God. Thus God will bless your service with *sustaining verification*.

For example, in response to God's spoken word through Peter and John, people were converted by the thousands (4:4), the lame miraculously experienced healing (4:10), the city was aroused (4:16), and the Jewish leaders arose in alarm and opposition (4:18). *But no one ignored the apostles!* To the contrary, even scoffers admitted "that indeed a notable miracle hath been done by them is manifest to all . . . and we cannot deny it" (4:16).

This is especially true in the case of the exercise of your spiritual gift. As I have stated, it is in this sense that gifts are signs, in that God has promised certain results as signs to verify your gift.

I believe the signs are listed in 1 Corinthians 12:8-10. This was never intended to be a comprehensive list, however, but suggestive of the kind of results you can expect. You are to look for results of the very same kind. The list suggests you look for very *definite, spiritual, practical, supernatural* results. These results should be evidenced in the lives of those to whom you minister, in terms of communicated insights, the motivation of them to action, and life-changing effects. These kinds of results will reveal you have truly discovered your gift (and the area of service in which you are to major). They will also sustain your interest in serving God.

For example, allow me to review the sequence of events which led me to the discovery of my own spiritual gift. And let me identify our five factors (although I did not realize them at the time).

During my junior year in college, I came to a place of intense and unconditional commitment of my life to Christ. After that, there were occasional detours in my spiritual journey. But, for the most part Christ had the controlling interest of my life.

In the days which followed, my life was supercharged with thrilling pulsations of newfound joy, peace, and purpose. I experienced the relief of a conscience cleansed of guilt and the wonder of a way of life that truly satisfied. I began to experience some profound changes in my life—all for the better. All this filled my heart with an abounding love for Christ and my fellowman. I soon found myself afire with a desire to serve him (Divine Inception). This desire compelled me to action (Intense Compulsion). And that desire clearly focused in one particular activity of service.

I developed a desire to stand and share his truth with others (Rational Selection). And my desire was insatiable. Where I had stubbornly spurned opportunities to speak before, now I found myself volunteering for every opportunity. I gave devotional talks for every Sunday School department at my church. I took every opportunity to speak at the various devotional gatherings for Christians on my campus. Soon I began teaching a Sunday School class of young boys. And I began giving my testimony in banquets, youth revivals, and church services in the surrounding areas (Decisive Acceptance).

Moreover, God blessed my verbal efforts with telling effect in the lives of others (Sustained Verification). God multiplied the results of my efforts far beyond my meager ability. Of course, these blessings further sustained my desire for speaking, and I later became an ordained minister. However, though I never questioned the source of motivation was God, it was years later that I recognized this aptitude as a "spiritual gift."

You see, God has led multitudes of Christians into successful Christian service along the line of his choosing for their lives . . . without their ever realizing they were exercising what the Bible calls a "spiritual gift." Perhaps you can now look back and recognize our five factors in your motivation to service, although you did not recognize them at the time of your experience.

How, then, do you discover your spiritual enablement? What can you do to find out just what your spiritual gift is?

It is all a matter of motivation. Seek such fullness of God's power in your life that he blesses you to the point that love compels you (a Divine Inception) with such intensity that you *have to* serve him (an Intense Compulsion), then step out on faith and select the area of service (in Romans 12) in which your desire centers (a Rational Selection) and make a definite, irrevocable commitment to begin exercising that gift, accepting it as your basic service responsibility (a Decisive Acceptance) wherein God will supernaturally enable your efforts (a Sustaining Verification)!

This formula provides the five foundational principles upon which the following Spiritual Aptitude Test will be based, and an understanding of them should carry you "right on" through the next chapter to the discovery of your service gift!

6

Your Spiritual Aptitude Test

God has a special purpose for your life. The Holy Spirit indwells a Christian life to *use* it. And the purpose of his indwelling is to powerfully enable you to serve in an area of God's choosing. We have traditionally referred to this as your spiritual gift in that God will mightily use you in this one special area of service. This is "where the action is" for you!

Obviously, then, the next step is to review the different areas in which a person can be gifted. They are listed for us in the twelfth chapter of Romans. Take a careful look at each one of them.

If you will value a spiritual gift as a pearl of great price and if you are willing to "sell out" to develop it, God will most likely reveal your gift as you prayerfully study these seven areas. You should see yourself distinctly in one of them. You will sense your enabling in that area. Ask the Holy Spirit for guidance and examine your life by each of them.

This study will serve as your Spiritual Aptitude Test.

Aptitude #1—Prophecy: "Not Fore, but Forth"

The word "prophecy" originates from the Hebrew *havi* and the Greek *propheter* which means *to speak in behalf of another*. In the Christian sense, a prophet speaks for God. If God has given you a supernatural enabling in this activity, you will have keen insight into the mind of God, coupled with the ability to communicate his thought to others. A prophet is God's "mouthpiece," his spokesman.

Prophecy does not refer to the ability to predict, tell fortunes, or any such crystal-ball gazing. Prophecy is more *forthtelling* than *foretelling!* It reveals the Father more than the future.

W. A. Criswell says of prophecy: "Only in the medieval times did the word pass into the English language in the sense of prediction." [1]

Whoever first labeled the TV weatherman a prophet might well have understood the word as it has meaning today. Each evening, as part of the nightly news program, the TV weatherman tells you how it is. That is, he steps forward into your television screen to report on the weather at home and across the nation. He reports on barometric pressures, the temperature, and identifies weather fronts that are sweeping the country. Basically, he is a *reporter*. He reports from authentic weathercasts that have been supplied to him from the official weather station. But he also takes a moment at the close of his report to offer a forecast of tomorrow's weather conditions. He looks at the present climate, draws from past records, and shares the impression he receives about the likelihood of showers tomorrow.

Prophecy resembles a weather report in that the prophet only tells what has been revealed to him from an authoritative source . . . God. A prophet is a spokesman for God. When a person steps forward to prophesy, he relates some word from God on the local spiritual climate; he identifies a current spiritual trend; or he points out some specific condition that needs attention. The New Testament purpose of prophecy is of a practical nature: "He that prophesieth speaketh unto men to edification, and exhortation, and comfort" (1 Cor. 14:3). A prophet delivers a message from God to man. And prophecy addresses itself to general spiritual needs of such practical value that it can be personally applied to your life. In this sense, a prophet is basically a reporter.

A prophet does *not* necessarily receive an original "revelation" of knowledge from heaven. God has already said most everything he intends to say to us in the Holy Scriptures, which are his words to man (2 Pet. 1:20). Most prophecy comes from inspiration and illuminated interpretation concerning the principles and passages of God's Word. Usually, it is on the basis of what we have learned of him in the Scriptures that God impresses us with what should be said!

However, I have been in "small group" gatherings where some spoke of receiving a prophecy as if it were something *"divined"* from God. I have known those who systematically interrupt a prayer session to reveal a "prophecy," something God told them to say . . . as if they had a "hot line" to heaven. Some claim to receive visions, which are interpreted as practical instruction for others. Such direct revelation, when it is *casually* or *constantly* provided, fills me with deep apprehension. Because I can instantly recall an endless number of heartrending decisions based on just this type of logic . . . a revelation someone took to be a direct word from God. I remember the boy in our youth group who burned down a dance hall. His only justification for this action was, "God told me to do it." I recall the friend who decided against seminary training, the boy who dropped out of college, the lady who attempted suicide, a man who left his wife for another woman, and the myriads of young people who married non-Christians . . . all to disastrous ends. But in each case they claimed, "God told me this is what I should do." And it was a leader in the charismatic movement, Bob Mumford, who said: "It is my own personal conviction that some seventy percent of our guidance comes through the written Word of God, approximately another twenty percent comes by the Holy Spirit speaking, and the last ten percent may come through dreams, visions, prophecy, or other direct signs." [2]

Don't misunderstand! I believe God *can* give you specific, personal instruction . . . *and give you a message for someone else.* The New Testament bears record of such instances, as when Peter received a message for the centurion (Acts 11:5-11) and when Ananias received instruction for Paul (Acts 9:6-16).

But such revelations are *rare, often erroneously claimed,* and *subject to gross misuse.* Satan is also a great one for impressing the mind.

Sermons are a classic mode of prophecy . . . as you share a word from God for today. If you are gifted in this activity, you will possess a unique ability to grasp the mind of God concerning spiritual matters, coupled with effectiveness in communicating your insight to others. And, as I have said, usually it is on the basis of what we have learned in the Scriptures that God impresses us with what he would have us say.

In any case, the pronouncement of a true prophet should bear the mark of fresh spiritual insight and practical personal value. Above all, he will be a communicator . . . and those who hear him will know they have received a word from heaven . . . a relevant word just for them. This is why it is so common for people, after having heard some godly prophet speak, to remark: "I felt he was talking just to me!"

But what about you? What is your spiritual aptitude? Remember, motivation is the key. Search your life with regard to the five factors of spiritual motivation. Test yourself by them:

Factor #1: Divine Inception

Does your spiritual experience with Christ result in thrilling revelations which you long to share with others?

Factor #2: Intense Compulsion

How intense is your motivation to speak for God? When asked to give a testimony or share a devotional thought . . . is there an inward thrill and excitement at the prospect? Is your longing to speak intense and lasting? (Perhaps a hyper-timid person or one with natural fear at speaking will have *mixed emotions* at this point. A part of him might fear the experience of speaking while another part of him will yearn to stand and speak!)

Factor #3: Natural Selection

Have you experienced a compulsion to proclaim the message of God. Be very honest at this point. Is your motivation a desire *to be heard* or a desire *to tell?* Does your desire arise from the value of the message you have received or the attention you get when sharing it?

Factor #4: Decisive Acceptance

Are you willing to irrevocably commit your life to the exercise of this gift?

Factor #5: Sustaining Verification

If you have experienced opportunities to speak for God, did the results verify your gift? Did things happen which took God to explain? Do "significant others" recognize your gift (it should be that obvious)? Perhaps persons were converted or lives transformed. Did people respond to a course of action? Were they moved? Were minds enlightened, hearts warmed, and wills challenged?

If you are inexperienced, seek every opportunity to speak. Do it by faith. Trust God to verify your gift along the lines of 2 Corinthians 12:8-10! This speaks of very *definite, spiritual, practical, supernatural* results in terms of communicated insights, the motivation of others to action, and life-changing effect!

Aptitude #2—Ministry: "Hooked On Service"

The word "ministry" means to *"render service"* (1 Pet. 4:11, Amplified). In a purely Christian sense it means sacrificial and effective service to others, exercised in the power of God.

If this is your gift, you will be a *doer*. Others may see needs and sit unmoved, but you will have a tendency to do something. You will be *task oriented* with a newfound willingness and ability to get things done. You will find yourself responding to tasks like metal to a magnet. While others who see the wreck of humanity merely stand by and stare, you will look around for something to repair!

The gift of ministry is so highly developed in some individuals that God can accomplish a myriad of vastly differing types of service. They keep numerous "irons in the fire" simultaneously.

However, I also recall a cherished man of God who exercised his gift of ministry in the splendid performance of *one* single task. For years and years he served as chairman of ushers in an active church, and the endless ways he found to help people through that one position of service still fills me with absolute amazement.

On a given Sunday, he might perform two dozen acts of ministry for as many different people, acts which might range from securing men to help a handicapped member in a wheelchair, introducing newcomers to a Christian real estate agent, notifying the pastor of special guests, and helping some child find a lost Bible. No one ever left a service ungreeted. Seldom was he caught unprepared for sudden unexpected needs. And he did it all so quietly, *he was seldom noticed!*

This gift can be recognized by *intuitive practical insights for meeting human need.* The Holy Spirit will have a way of opening your eyes to the practical steps to take for meeting different needs. A vital aspect of a gift of ministry is the "sanctified common sense" to do the best thing in a given situation in the most effective manner. A Christian so gifted won't come within a country mile of being mistaken for a busybody who always pries into other people's affairs! Indeed, it is Spirit-imparted, practical wisdom about human needs which will compel your heart to active concern!

But what about you? Have you experienced God working through the five stages of motivation in order to exercise this spiritual gift through your life? If so, you should be able to recognize:

Factor #1: A Divine Inception

Has your spiritual experience with Christ issued in a restless urge to do something about the needs of our world? Does your practical insight into the way to meet needs compel you to be a doer?

Factor #2: Intense Compulsion

How intense is your motivation? Must people coax you to help, or is your response to tasks spontaneous? Is there something within you that propels you toward an undone task? Are you happiest when you are busy accomplishing something? Do you seem more active than others? Do you enjoy a task well done? Do you tend to accept when asked to do something?

Factor #3: Natural Selection

Suppose a small boy walked up to you in the foyer of your church after a morning worship service. What if he tells you he can't find his Bible. What would your reaction be? Would your first reaction be to call for an usher, refer him to the "lost and found" table, or go help him find it? Those with this gift would likely do the latter.

Factor #4: Decisive Acceptance

Will you accept this gift as your basic service responsibility and "sell out" for the development of it?

Factor #5: Sustained Verification

If this is your gift, God will verify it by blessing your deeds of service with the kind of results listed in 1 Corinthians 12:8-10. Do your good deeds have a way of blessing folks beyond explanation? Do you find lasting satisfaction through your service? Does God bless your efforts in a definite and telling manner? Does your effort influence and encourage others to join in? Do others recognize this gift in you?

My wife was typical of most girls when she was young, petted but seldom pampered, and in no way precocious. She was one step ahead of me all the time and I never realized it—until I was saying "I do!" Actually, we dated for years before we married. She had the most uncanny ability to keep me interested while keeping a diversionary tactic ready if I began to come on too strong. She had all the finesse of a Spanish bullfighter who sidesteps a rampaging bull with an effortless flip of his cape. She had mastered the art of playing "hard to get," and I kept chasing her until *she caught me.*

In our later years of dating I witnessed a marvelous transformation in her life. Somewhere her affection matured into genuine love. Then I saw that love begin to draw her out of the confines of her own life to live within the circumference of mine, which had become almost dearer to her than her own. After marriage, I witnessed her further loss of self consideration and marvelled how she could orbit around my life. She became a perfect "help-mate" while maintaining her own identify and individuality in the inexplicable service rendered me. Then came our children, and I witnessed anew that the limit of a godly woman's love is endless in terms of sacrificial service. At present she teaches our children on the road, directs a diversified children's program during the conferences at night, maintains our home when off the road, keeps herself and the girls immaculate, types all our correspondence, not to mention sewing and caring for a husband who is all thumbs. She is spiritually gifted in the realm of ministry.

Aptitude #3—Teaching: "To Tell the Truth"

God blesses some people with a supernatural enduement for teaching spiritual truths. Such a person will relish opportunities when they can teach, as did Jesus when he opened "their understanding, that they might understand the scriptures" (Luke 24:45).

The gift of teaching can be identified by several definite characteristics. First, those who have the gift of teaching will receive spiritual illumination into the meaning of the Scriptures. The Holy Spirit will enlighten their minds with unusual clarity of insight. To borrow an analogy from Sidlow Baxter, it is much like those rows of reflectorized posts on the highway which mark dangerous bends on the road. The reflectors are hardly noticeable in the daytime, but at night they flash out brilliantly when caught in the headlights of a car. By parallel, this is what happens when a "gifted" teacher goes through the Bible under the illumination of the Holy Spirit. Again and again, that which is missed by others lights up with living significance. There is a verse which describes instruction by a gifted teacher: "Which things also we speak, not in words which man's wisdom teacheth, but which the

Spirit teacheth, interpreting spiritual things to spiritual men" (1 Cor. 2:13, ASV).

The difference between the spiritual illumination of the "gifted" teacher and the Spirit's guidance of every Christian is one of *degree*. The spiritual gift in the realm of teaching is evidenced by unusually penetrating divine insight.

Secondly, the gift of teaching will also manifest itself in an obsessive intellectual thirst for a practical grasp of the Bible as a whole (although the gifted person need not necessarily be either brilliant of mind or broad in formal education). He will desire to study the Bible extensively and systematically. He will respond to the biblical command to *search* (explore, research) the Scriptures (John 5:39). He will look for the occasional jewel of truth, like the prophet; but he will also search out everything else contained in the mine. Sidlow Baxter has well said:

> Illumination by the Holy Spirit must never be thought of as a substitute for diligent and methodical *study* of the Bible. Not only are there latent meanings which only the Spirit-illumined perceive, but there are sub-surface coincidences, singularities, confirmations, and other "finds," which yield only for those who *search*.[3]

The spiritual gift of teaching will include the hunger for study that pays the price for a "philosopher's grasp" of the entire scope of biblical revelation.

The gift of teaching will not only be· evidenced by illuminated interpretation and systematic search but, thirdly, by *clear communication* of the Scriptures. Even though the gifted teacher addresses the logical faculties of his hearers and will likely follow a carefully prepared sequence of thought, his teaching will be anointed of the Spirit with explosive effect. The truth he shares will change people.

I was reared in a little town called Nacogdoches, Texas. We had a lady there in my home church who had the spiritual gift of teaching. Her name: Miss Sally T. Summers. She never married, taught music as her vocation, but devoted her entire life to teaching the Bible. While I was a college student, some fifteen fellows gathered in the home of her and her brother. We met one night each week for a year. She taught us the Gospel of John. That group of young men are serving

God all over the nation, bearing the fruit of her teaching. I have often wondered just how many lives have been transformed through the teaching of this one woman. Yet she always remained in relative insignificance. She was the most *modest, pure,* and *sensitive* lady I have ever known. Never in my life have I heard her make a critical remark about another person, nor do I ever recall hearing anyone make a critical remark about her. She was not an aggressive person, but when she taught the Bible, there was not only *clarity,* but *fire, force,* and *compelling power.*

I would venture to say that a church Sunday School staffed with teachers like this would transform a congregation within one year. How blessed you are if this is your gift!

What about it? Have you experienced God working through the five stages of spiritual motivation in order to exercise this spiritual gift through you? If so, you should be able to recognize:

Factor #1: A Divine Inception

Has God given you an insatiable hunger for the Scriptures, coupled with penetrating insights into its meaning? Are these insights exciting to share?

Factor #2: An Intense Compulsion

Has a longing for knowledge of the Scriptures compelled you to hours of study? Do you seem to study the Bible much more than the average Christian around you? Do you have a love for resource books which enrich your knowledge?

Factor #3: A Natural Selection

Do you glean all your spiritual truths from the many excellent Christian books of our day, or have you also developed a habit of studying the Scriptures for yourself? Have you an obsessive intellectual thirst for a practical grasp of the Bible as a whole? Do you read the Scriptures devotionally *and* study for the full meaning of the Scriptures systematically?

Factor #4: Decisive Acceptance

Will you accept the task of teaching as your major responsibility and devote yourself to it . . . unceasingly?

Factor #5: Sustaining Verification

Have you taught the Scriptures enough to note that something happens in the lives of others when you teach? Do they receive some word of knowledge and wisdom that thrills them with what they have learned? Does your teaching actually affect the lives of others? Do others recognize your gift of teaching?

Aptitude #4—Exhortation: "A Manner of Speaking"

Exhortation is translated from the Greek word *parakaleo*. It is a vital word, describing an aspect of spiritual experience that is little understood and grossly unappreciated.

Very honestly, I have explored this spiritual gift with a sense of awe and amazement. In eighteen years as a pastor, I cannot honestly remember making more than a casual reference to this activity. Yet, in searching the Scriptures, I am dumbfounded to find it was a potent, indispensable practice among the early believers. How much we have missed in neglecting it. How much we need to restore it in the daily practice of Christian experience.

What is exhortation? Exhortation is a *manner* of speaking with others. When you exhort, you speak in such a manner as to move someone to action: "To exhort and convince the gainsayers" (Titus 1:9). Notice in the following verses, people are exhorted to *do* something:

"exhorted them all, that . . . they would cleave" (Acts 11:23);
"exhorting them to continue" (Acts 14:22);
"exhorted . . . that you would walk" (1 Thess. 2:11-12);
"we exhort you, brethren, warn them" (1 Thess. 5:14);
"I exhort . . . that . . . prayers . . . be made" (1 Tim. 2:1);
"exhort to be sober minded" (Titus 2:6).

To exhort is to verbally motivate another person. Indeed, the word is often translated *beseech* (Phil. 4:2; 1 Pet. 2:11; and many other verses). It is not so much a prophecy as it is a *plea;* not so much a *sermon* as it is a *supplication.*

When you exhort, you also speak in a warm, very personal, almost intimate manner. The original Greek word *parakaleo* is derived from two words which mean "to call to one's side." Thus we have the root meaning of calling someone to come sit by your side for counsel! The Bible explicitly states you should exhort in a personal way "as a father doth his children" (1 Thess. 2:11). In another passage the Bible says,

"Rebuke not an elder, but intreat him as a father" (1 Tim. 5:1). The word *intreat* here is actually the same word elsewhere translated "exhort."

The Amplified Bible rightly expanded the meaning of the word to include: "Urged and warned and consoled and encouraged" (Acts 15:32). This is what you do when you exhort.

Another thing about exhortation, your manner of expression should usually be *conversation*, one person counseling another: "But exhort one another" (Heb. 10:25). The Bible does speak of *written* exhortation, "I have written briefly . . . exhorting" (1 Pet. 5:12). The Bible also refers to *sermonic* exhortation: "And many other things in this exhortation preached he unto the people" (Luke 3:18). However, if exhortation is a part of preaching, it usually refers to one aspect of preaching: that of personal entreaty. Exhortation should usually be practiced on a one-to-one basis; it is a *daily* activity: "But exhort one another daily" (Heb. 3:13).

Therefore, it can be said that exhortation is one person counseling with another in order to move them to action by warmly urging, warning, consoling, and encouraging . . . and it should be the daily practice of Christian believers!

If the Holy Spirit has chosen you for the exercise of this service gift, your life will take on an affinity for people. You will find a strange drawing away from yourself. *You will begin to love enough to be personally involved in the lives of others.* The gifts of prophecy, ministry, teaching, giving, and ruling are all aimed at helping others, but at arm's length—not in a way as to be so personally involved in their lives. You will begin to know something about the compassionate heart which moved Paul to say, "I have great heaviness and continual sorrow in my heart . . . for my brethren" (Rom. 9:2-3). And you will care enough to confront your brethren in a very personal manner.

Some will exercise this gift most often as "soul-winners," confronting non-Christians with a reconciling gospel. But I have known many who have excelled in their ability to counsel and encourage wayward Christians who also need reconciliation to God, to others, and within themselves.

If this is your gift, our world waits laggard and thin-ranked for the rallying impact of your life! But again we must focus on you, personally. Have you experienced God working through the five stages of motivation in order to exercise this spiritual gift through your life? Have you experienced:

Factor #1: A Divine Inception

Has God begun to care and reach out to others through your life? Do you have a newfound compassion for people? Are you *soul-conscious* . . . that is, are you aware of people and their needs? Do you have a deep desire for God to touch the lives of other people through you?

Factor #2: An Intense Compulsion

Has your concern for others moved you to action . . . have you learned to be a soul-winner . . . or involved yourself in counseling opportunities? Does God seem to give you that sixth sense, a sanctified common sense with regard to human nature? Do you feel guilty when you fail to tell someone what you know they need to hear?

Factor #3: Natural Selection

Do you really enjoy personal confrontations with others? Have you been so consistently helpful to others that *people often seek you out for counsel?* What kind of activities grab your heart most readily—those related to programs, projects, or people? The latter is indicative of this gift.

Factor #4: Decisive Acceptance

Will you unreservedly and unceasingly commit yourself to this "people-conscious" ministry?

Factor #5: A Sustaining Verification

Have you been noticeably effective in winning others to Christ? Has God given you that "personal touch" with people—the ability to establish rapport and counsel in such a way as to move them to action? Are there souls God has used you to rescue, wayward lives you have been used to lead back on course? Do others recognize this gift in you?

The *full* effect of this spiritual gift in the life of a man is a marvel to behold. Samuel Grafflin used to tell of a man who lived out his life in a small mid-Western town. He was an inconspicuous man with little education. But he was one of the town's first citizens. Everyone called him "Joe," and when he would pray in church, something happened in people's hearts. He lived in a small house on a back street, but people made their way there constantly for that intangible something that puts hope into life. Samuel Grafflin tells about the day Joe died. The stores did little business that day. There was a hush in the streets. The wealthiest man in town brought his new carriage for Joe's widow to use. The florist denuded his greenhouse of its choicest flowers and flooded the little funeral parlor with beauty. The county undertaker drove fifteen miles over the hills to offer his service, free. He said, "I was a drunkard on those roads until one day Joe got hold of me and told me of the saving grace of Christ." And so they came. The old toll-gate keeper said, "I've been keeping this toll gate for thirty-five years now, but never before have I seen twelve hundred carriages come from all over the county to pay tribute to one man." Such was the impact of one who cared enough to exhort others . . and did so in the power of God!

Aptitude #5—Giving: "Beyond the Call of Duty"

Another activity in which some will receive a special gift is in the area of giving: "He that giveth" here is translated from the Greek word *metadidōmi*. It is important to note this is not the normal word for "giving" used elsewhere in the New Testament because it means more than a simple contribution. *It is a compounded form of the more general word,* and it takes on a larger meaning: "to give of oneself." It is the New Testament equivalent of the Old Testament phrase, "spirit of might" (Isa. 11:2), a phrase indicating how the Holy Spirit would move upon a leader to give of himself in costly, heroic action.

In terms of service today, this enabling refers to an ability to lose yourself in a reckless abandon for others. It speaks of heroic action. The Congressional Medal of Honor is conferred for service "above and beyond the call of duty." Some people can do the *big* thing—they can pour their life into a cause. Such a person can inspire boundless effort from others. No one has given of himself in costly service more heroically than Paul, who once recounted: "Five different times the Jews gave me their terrible thirty-nine lashes. Three times I was beaten with rods. Once I was stoned. Three times I was shipwrecked. . . . I have traveled many weary miles and have been often in great danger from flooded rivers and from robbers. . . . I have faced grave dangers from mobs in the cities and from death in the deserts and in the stormy seas" (2 Cor. 11:24-26, TLB).

This speaks of a Martin Luther, nailing his theses to the door and spawning the Reformation—yes, and a Martin Luther King who lays down his life for "civil rights." History records the men who hazard their lives in such a way as to move other men for a cause. Such men are super-normal—they have great facility for giving. Such are they who exercise their spiritual gift . . . in the sense of Christian service.

I recall the statement of an old foreign missionary to Africa. He had given his life for Nigeria, and his deeds were legend among the African people. But he was also very weary. And, as he thought of those years of sacrifice in comparison with so many easy-living Christians in America, he said: "It has always amazed me that God expects so much from so few, and so little from so many." But I think he missed the point. *The truth is that God motivates a few beyond the little of so many in order to have his heroes in the faith!*

But what about you? Have you experienced God working through the five stages of motivation in order to exercise this spiritual gift through your life? Have you experienced:

Factor #1: A Divine Inception

Has God given you the inner drive to surmount and succeed for the cause of Christ? Does God seem to expect more of you than others? Do you often find that you give of yourself more than others?

Factor #2: An Intense Compulsion

Are you the kind of Christian who gets *totally* involved if you are involved at all? Do you have a tendency to go "all out" for a cause? Are you motivated with a sense of desperate urgency about the cause of Christ? When involved in Christian service, are you the *first to arrive,* the *last to leave,* and the *least likely to quit?*

Factor #3: A Natural Selection

Do you always find yourself giving more than is expected in God's service? Do you get your greatest enjoyment from a deep-rooted involvement in some cause of Christ?

Factor #4: Decisive Acceptance

Will you be willing to lose yourself in a reckless abandon for others

. . . regardless of the cost?

Factor #5: A Sustaining Verification

Does God give you a "second wind" in service so that you always seem to go the farthest in giving yourself for a cause? Does your effort often result in miraculous accomplishment? Are others amazed by the extent of your giving?

Aptitude #6—Ruling: "God's Invincibles"

The word *rule* is translated from the Greek word *proistamenos*, and it means to stand before, to preside, to be over.

From the beginning of his dealing with men, God has chosen to use some as rulers or leaders in accomplishing spiritual goals. It was so in the life of Israel. Sometimes He called Moses to lead the entire nation (Ex. 3:10). But lesser rulers were also a part of his design, for after calling Moses to be ruler of Israel he further instructed him to select several ranks of lesser leadership: "Moreover thou shalt provide out of all the people *able men . . .* and place such over them, *to be rulers of thousands, and rulers of hundreds, and rulers of fifties, and rulers of tens"* (Ex. 18:21, italics added).

God bestows a special gift of leadership upon those who should lead or rule. But what is this gift? What sets some men apart? What is the underlying factor that causes some men and women to be selected to places of leadership? Where do men get the strength to lead? Why is it some very unlikely men are successful spiritual leaders?

Without hesitancy, I say the key to the door of successful spiritual leadership *is a sense of divine authority which comes with a call from God for each task.* The authority of a leader is his standard equipment; the rest of his natural qualities will vary greatly from the simple to the complex. A Christian leader may or may not have a college degree or a strong church background. He may or may not possess a grand manner, a handsome appearance, or that illusive quality commonly referred to as a "good personality." He may or may not possess some of the more intricate qualities such as independence in judgment, mental flexibility (an ability to adjust quickly to new developments), the ability to abstract (proficiency in breaking down problems into their component parts), or the ability to synthesize (the skills to combine several elements in a creative manner to form a whole). In fact, apart from the hand of God upon his life, he might be referred to as "clever," or he might be called "common." But the one vital quality which will set him apart as a leader is a sense of divine authority for his task . . . which originates from the call of God. A leader might have little else; but if, deep down, he knows that God has called him to a task, he will stay at it until God has accomplished his purpose. And God will always come through, in his own way!

But every leader in God's service *must* have a definite call from God for the particular task at which he is engaged. This is mandatory. Alan Redpath is quite correct. If God has chosen you for a particular task that requires you to be selected by your fellowman, he will move upon their hearts and lead them to you. But he will always validate that selection by issuing a personal call to you. Indeed, he will hunt you up like a lightning flash!

A classic example of this is seen in Moses' *two* attempts to lead Israel out of their Egyptian bondage.

Moses failed in his first attempt to deliver the Israelites from their slavery in Egypt. He made the mistake of trying to lead without a call: "*He supposed* his brethren would have understood how that God by His hand would deliver them" (Acts 7:25, italics added). But *supposition* is not a call. Void of divine authority in his leadership, Moses failed to gain the following of the people, who resisted him, saying: "Who made thee a ruler over us" (Acts 7:27).

However, forty years later God *did* call Moses to lead Israel out of Egypt: "This Moses whom they refused, saying, Who made thee a ruler . . . the same did God send to be a ruler and a deliverer" (Acts 7:35).

But this time Moses had learned his lesson well. This time he would not budge until he was assured of God's specific call (Ex. 3:10-15). Moses reminded God of Israel's former unwillingness to follow him and asked what *authority* he would have. God responded by giving him authority to use his shepherd's rod to work the miracles of God . . . but the *authority of that rod was in the call of God to use it!* Victory soon followed. As Alan Redpath once said: "Therefore, in relation to any duties which you would undertake for God, I want

to say very earnestly that the supreme question is not 'Are you quali-
fied?,' but 'Are you called?' Are you grasping for position, or are you
called of God? Answer that to the Lord in his presence." [4] What about
you? Have you experienced God working through the five stages of
motivation in order to exercise this spiritual gift through your life?
Have you experienced:

Factor #1: A Divine Inception

Has your total commitment to Christ and the ensuing desire for service
been met with a "call" to leadership in some Christian endeavor?

Factor #2: An Intense Compulsion

Perhaps your call to leadership came in terms of your being asked
to direct a Sunday School department, a youth group, a new building
drive, or some spiritual task force from your church. In each case beware
of the "drum-major instinct," for we all have wanted to lead the band.
Did you respond to a definite, clear, intense impression from God,
or do you simply want to be No. 1? Are you the kind of person who
would never volunteer but would sit back and formulate a plan . . .
and could work the plan if called upon to do so?

Factor #3: Natural Selection

Has God verified your call to leadership by opening doors of opportunity and leading others to select you for some task? Are you the kind
of person who could organize a tornado?

Factor #4: Decisive Acceptance

Will you accept your responsibility and stay at it until the task is
completed, no matter what the cost?

Factor #5: A Sustaining Verification

Has God blessed your leadership with accomplishments like those
of 1 Corinthians 12? Was your effort of such magnitude that Satan
opposed you? Did God accomplish his purposes? Do others consider
you a leader?

Aptitude #7—Showing Mercy: "Pity Plus Action"

The word *mercy* is translated from the Greek word *eleos*. It means
to feel sympathy with the misery of another, especially such sympathy
as manifests itself in action. Whereas the Greek synonym of this word,
oikteirō, means a feeling of compassion that is kept within, on the

other hand, *eleos* means a sense of pity plus effort to relieve the suffering. As Lloyd-Jones affirms, "that is the essential meaning of being merciful; it is *pity* plus action." [5] I like to think of mercy as love in action on behalf of someone in misery.

A spiritual gift for this activity, then, would involve supernatural ability to empathize and care when someone is in need, to *identify* with them in their need, plus the inner drive to untiringly work to help them through their plight.

L. O. Johnson once said there are three levels of *caring*. All Christians should care enough to be *inconvenienced*. This is the first level of caring, and it means you are touchable; you are willing to be bothered; you are subject to call and will go out of your way. Even if it taxes your strength and resources, you are willing to be inconvenienced in order to help someone in need.

Beyond merely caring enough to be inconvenienced, others will care enough to be *involved*. That's the second level of caring. Those who receive the "gift of exhortation" will care on this deeper level. This means you care enough to do more than just help from afar, "at arm's length." You will care enough to want to be personally involved with people.

In contrast, then, the gift of showing mercy is response on a deeper level. If you have this gift, God will enable you to care enough to be *identified*. This is caring at its deepest level, both in terms of what you *feel* and what you *do* about the misery of another. To "identify" is to see another's misery *as if it were your own*. His pain becomes your pain; his need becomes your need; his sorrow becomes your sorrow . . . even if for only a while, at least long enough to move you to sustained action.

It is not natural for anyone to care like that. It is not within our human nature to care that deeply. We came into this world created *equal* before God, but we are not created *identical*. There are vast differences between us—individual differences in color, race, size, sex, temperament, ability, ideals, goals, cultures, needs, environment, interests, attitudes, religions, looks, and stations of life. And we spend our lives trying to bridge these gaps between us. But some have a supernatural ability to do so, at least when someone is in need. He who has the gift of mercy will identify with the need as if it were his own.

I was riding in an automobile with a pastor in Houma, Louisiana, when he pointed to another car which was pulling into a grocery store parking lot. He remarked: "Do you see the lady who is driving that car? She is exercising that gift of mercy you spoke about in the conference this morning. There are four elderly widows in our city, and she picks each one of them up separately to spend some time with them and take them out in her car to care for all their errands. She does it each and every week."

But what about you? Have you experienced God working through the five stages of motivation in order to exercise this spiritual gift in your life? Have you experienced:

Factor #1: A Divine Inception

Has your Christian experience produced a deep sensitivity to people in need? Do you feel the pain and need of others?

Factor #2: An Intense Compulsion

Do you feel the pain of others enough to *spontaneously* respond to their need (pity plus action)? Do you seem to care more than others? Do you care enough to identify?

Factor #3: A Natural Selection

Suppose you were on a trip in your automobile and came upon an accident. You stop your car and run over to the scene of the accident. Once there, you discover a car had skidded off the road into a ditch and a body was lying by the road. Would your first impulse be to stop another car and send for police or kneel beside the body and tend to his wound? The merciful would be most inclined to do the latter! Do you feel real compassion toward those you find in need?

Factor #4: Decisive Acceptance

Will you accept this responsibility as your basic service task . . . and unswervingly commit yourself!

Factor #5: A Sustaining Verification

Has God touched and blessed the lives of people through you? Has He met their needs? Have the signs of 1 Corinthians 12 resulted from your deeds? Do others recognize this gift in you?

So, there you have a description of the seven areas in which God will supernaturally enable you for service. Remember, the secret to developing your spiritual gift is the *"sell-out principle."* You must consider your gift a pearl of great price. You must recognize it as an enabling of such value as to be worth sacrificing all your natural gifts for. Sell out in your commitment to it.

John Baillie captured the spirit of the matter when he told of an experience which took place long ago in the northwest frontier of India. A troop of robbers came upon a man leading a fine horse. "Where are you going?" they demanded!

"I am taking this *horse* to my master's son as a gift."

The robbers beat the man, left him, but carried off the horse.

Later in the day the man fell in with another band of thieves who likewise asked him, "Where are you going?"

"I carry to my master's son a gift of a *gold chain.*"

The robbers searched him and found the chain concealed in his turban. They took the chain and most of his clothes, but let him go.

At last the man reached his destination and presented himself to his master's son who, seeing a limping, footsore man wearing only a ragged loincloth, looked upon him with astonishment. But the man approached to say, "I bring the master's son a gift." So saying, he took from his armpit the great *pearl*, now called the Mountain of Milk, which to this day is most illustrious among the treasures of the Amirs of that land.[6]

If the Lord returns tomorrow, would he find you with your gift?

Notes

1. W. A. Criswell, *The Holy Spirit in Today's World* (Grand Rapids: Zondervan Publishing House, 1966), p. 135.

2. Bob Mumford, *Take Another Look at Guidance* (Plainfield, New Jersey: Logos International, 1971), p. 75.

3. J. Sidlow Baxter, *The Strategic Grasp of the Bible* (Grand Rapids: Zondervan Publishing House, 1968), p. 33.

4. Alan Redpath, *Victorious Christian Living* (Westwood, New Jersey: Fleming H. Revell Co., 1955), p. 30.

5. D. Martin Lloyd-Jones, *Studies in the Sermon on the Mount* (Grand Rapids: Wm. B. Eerdmans Publishing Co., 1959), I, 99.

6. John Baillie, *Christian Devotion* (New York: Charles Scribner's Sons, 1962), pp. 68-69.

7

A New Look at Spiritual Gifts

At the risk of an overemphasis on this one subject, let us take one more look at what the Bible actually teaches about spiritual gifts. Take a fresh, new look.

Every Christian has a spiritual gift. You do not seek a gift. You already have it. *"As every man hath received the gift,* even so minister the same one to another" (1 Pet. 4:10, italics added).

At your conversion, when the Holy Spirit came to indwell, he entered to carry out a special work through your life. He is already present and ready to use you, especially in one or two areas of service (some Christians have more than one gift). Now, your gift for service may lie dormant if you never intelligently cooperate with the Spirit's ministry through your life in the area of his choosing. But each Christian has a gift, and "God's gifts . . . are irrevocable. He never withdraws them when once they are given" (Rom. 11:29, Amplified).

Moreover, there is a diversity of gifts. The gifts of the Spirit vary. Not everyone receives the same gift. *But what so many fail to realize is that there is also a diversity of ways to administrate (execute) your gift as well as a diversity of operations (effects or results of your gift).* For this, let us turn to the Scriptures.

There is only one place in the Scriptures where the subject of spiritual gifts is formally discussed. Paul begins the twelfth chapter of 1 Corinthians with the announcement of this subject: "Now concerning spiritual gifts" (1 Cor. 12:1).

It is imperative to realize that the one most vital passage of Scripture concerning the gifts of the Spirit is in the opening verses of that chapter (1 Cor. 12:4-6). To neglect or ignore these distinctive and decisive verses is to shun the *one scriptural key* to a practical understanding of spiritual gifts! But with these verses as the central truth, all the various other biblical references to gifts will naturally fall into place: "Now there are diversities of *gifts,* but the same Spirit. And there are differences of *administrations,* but the same Lord. And there are diversities of *operations,* but it is the same God which worketh all in all" (1 Cor. 12:4-6, italics added). Please note there are *three distinct and separate terms in this passage.* It speaks of *gifts (charismata), administrations, (diakonion),* and *operations (energemata).* These three terms reveal *separate aspects* of spiritual gifts. To understand each aspect is to know what spiritual gifts are. They form three parts of one whole.

Spiritual Gifts Include a Variety of ENABLINGS

In our key passage, verse 4 states, "Now there are . . . *gifts.*" The word *gifts* is translated from the Greek word *charismaton.* This Greek word refers to *extraordinary enabling power.* One translation renders spiritual gifts as "special endowments of supernatural energy." In essence, as we have previously stated, a spiritual gift is a supernatural enabling in the realm of service.

Furthermore, God bestows an enabling power for service in a variety of areas. But there is one passage of Scripture that lists all the different areas. The passage opens with the statement "Having then *gifts differing*" (Rom. 12:6, italics added); then it goes on to list seven different areas of service in which God will supernaturally enable you: prophecy, ministry, teaching, exhorting, giving, ruling, showing mercy. (See Rom. 12:6-8.)

Each of these seven areas has been defined in our previous chapter. Let me reemphasize the fact that I believe there *are* only seven areas in which you are supernaturally enabled. It is my firm conviction that all the other scriptural passages concerning this subject either refer to the *execution* of your enabling power or the *effect* of it (as we shall see). Romans 6 provides the only scriptural delineation of the different areas in which you are enabled, *and your spiritual gift will be a supernatural enablement in one of these seven areas!*

Let me digress just long enough to see our seven spiritual gifts from the perspective of the whole Bible. You see, spiritual gifts are the "manifestation of the Spirit" (1 Cor. 12:7), and the Spirit has been carrying out his activities throughout the ages. Let me examine the manifestation of the Spirit as recorded in the Old Testament, the manifestation of the Spirit through the Savior, and the manifestation of spiritual gifts in New Testament times. The Spirit carries out seven major activities in each case.

In the Old Testament the Holy Spirit "came upon" men with power to do divinely-imposed work effectively. In Isaiah 11 you will find a list of the seven manifestations of the Spirit in the Old Testament, and the same passage prophesies that these manifestations will find expression in the coming Messiah: "And the (1) Spirit of the Lord shall rest upon him, (2) the Spirit of wisdom and (3) understanding, (4) the spirit of counsel and (5) might, (6) the spirit of knowledge and (7) fear of the Lord (Isa. 11:2, numbers added).

The following chart will provide an abbreviated overview of the seven activities of the Holy Spirit in terms of Christian service. We have listed the seven manifestations of the Holy Spirit in the Old Testament (as listed in Isa. 11), as each found expression in the Savior, and as each activity is now manifested through the saints. (See chart on page 88.)

The Bible teaches that the gifts of the Spirit are endowments of special ability along the seven routes of service.

Spiritual Gifts Include a Variety of EXECUTIONS

In our key passage, verse 5 states, "and there are . . . *administrations*." The word *administrations* is translated from the Greek word *diakonion*. It means "executing for the common good of others." So this phrase speaks of the various ways of *executing* your enabling power.

So there are not only various kinds of supernatural *enablings;* there are also various ways in which you should *execute* your enabling power. And the way to execute your gift is a matter of divine selection. You are responsible for seeking his divine leadership concerning the way to execute your enabling power. Indeed, the administration or execution of your enablement is a vital part of your spiritual gift. It further determines what your gift is, and it establishes the manner in which your gift will be exercised! The Lord will supernaturally empower your gift only as it is executed in the way he chooses.

Having mentioned this matter in verse 5, Paul actually reveals some

Manifestations of the Spirit	Manifested in the Savior	Manifested through the Saints
1. *"Spirit of the Lord"*—The Targum explains this as the spirit of prophecy. Example: "The Spirit of the Lord is upon me; because the Lord hath anointed me to preach good tidings" (Isa. 61:1).	1. As manifested in Jesus: "Jesus of Nazareth, which was a prophet mighty in deed and word" (Luke 24:19).	1. Manifested today by the gift of *prophecy.*
2. *"Spirit of Wisdom"*—Hebrew meaning: "a rare capacity for good judgment and the ability to put it to good use" in practical service.	2. As manifested in Jesus: "Whence hath this man this wisdom, and these mighty works" (Matt. 13:54).	2. Manifested today by the gift of *ministry.*
3. *"Spirit of Understanding"*—Refers to enlightened insight.	3. As manifested in Jesus: "Then opened he their understanding." (Luke 24:45).	3. Manifested today by the gift of *teaching.*
4. *"Spirit of Counsel"*—Refers to an ability to advise and encourage.	4. As manifested in Jesus: "His name shall be called Counsellor" (Isa. 9:6).	4. Manifested today by the gift of *exhortation.*
5. *"Spirit of Might"*—Refers to the ability to give yourself in heroic action.	5. As manifested in Jesus: "Who loved me, and gave himself for me" (Gal. 2:20).	5. Manifested today by the gift of *giving.*
6. *"Spirit of Knowledge"*—Refers to knowledge of men.	6. As manifested in Jesus: "He knew all men . . . what was in man" (John 2:24-25).	6. Manifested today by the gift of *ruling.*
7. *"Spirit of the fear of the Lord"*—Speaks of a sensitive heart, theopposite of hardness. (Isa. 63:17).	7. As manifested in Jesus: "Jesus wept" (John 11:35).	7. Manifested today by the gift of *showing mercy.*

different ways of executing your gift later in the same chapter: "And God hath set some in the church, first *apostles*, secondarily *prophets*, thirdly *teachers*, after that *miracles*, then gifts of *healing, helps, governments*, diversities of *tongues*" (1 Cor. 12:28, italics added).

In a sense, these verses do not speak about God's gift to the *individual* but God's gift to the *church*. Paul is setting forth examples here of ways God has suggested for you to execute your gift through a local church.

In contrast, these do not refer to the areas in which you are spiritually gifted, but they refer to the way you are to execute your gifts through the church. This list was not exhaustive. (The function of the evangelist was not listed in Corinthians, while it was a part of another list set forth in Ephesians.) These were examples, and "tongue-speech" was mentioned as a function only because it was a problem in Corinth at that time. In fact, it appears Paul is simply suggesting some functions that are a very natural corollary to the seven areas in which we are spiritually enabled for service, as recorded in Romans 12. The following is the list of areas in which you are enabled and the various *executions* showing how they would naturally relate to each area:

Areas Gifted (Rom. 12)	Ways to Execute Gifts (1 Cor. 12:28)
Prophecy	Can function as Apostles (Missionaries) or as Prophets.
Ministry	Can function as helpers.
Teaching	Can function as teachers.
Exhortation	Can function as evangelists.
Giving (of yourself)	Can function as miracle workers.
Ruling	Can function in government (leadership).
Showing Mercy	Can function as seekers of healing.

Again, I did not list tongue-speech in the column to the right because it does not seem to match up with anything in the left column. That is as I have said—Paul was just giving examples, and "tongue-speech" was added only because it was a problem in Corinth at the time! And he mentioned it *last* because of its rare occurrence (as has been the case throughout Christian history).

At the least, Paul is saying you should execute your service gift in various ways—the most obvious, practical, sensible way possible—exercising them in and through a local church. *At the most,* Paul is suggesting some definite standard functions in the church through which you are to exercise your gift.

But let me go one step further and list some specific tasks by which some laymen have executed their gift:

Prophet: Speak at jail services, street services, nursing homes, revivals in unchurched areas, services at mission points, vesper services in resort areas, as a Gideon, lay revival speaker, or men's brotherhood speaker, and so forth.

Helpers: Endless help in mission tasks, benevolent activities, disabled and handicapped, landscaping, transportation for elderly, driver or mechanic in bus ministry, and endless number of activities that require "Indians" as well as "chiefs."

Teachers: Stimulate good book reading, teaching Sunday School, teach Bible classes at nursing home, fire stations, mission Sunday School; and Bible studies at airports, for various industrial groups, in ladies' Koffee-Klatches, and so forth.

Evangelistic: Distributing literature at hotel lobbies, terminals, etc., personal evangelism, mobile-home ministry, child evangelism, summer camp counselor, evangelistic film ministry, jail visitation, coffee house evangelism, hospital visitation evangelism, juvenile police counseling, man the phone at crisis hot lines, bus visitation.

Miracle Worker: Develop a strong tape ministry, establish a city-wide crusade, establish a mission to migrants, or resort ministry, a retreat place, a ministry of foster care or a nursery school, establish a great bus ministry, Christian baby-sitting ministry.

Leadership: Lead out in laymen programs, youth work, auxiliary programs for youth, small-group efforts, interdenominational prayer groups, lay retreat leadership and lay-renewal conference leaders, a project to minister to alcoholics, etc.

Healing: Minister to the sick, the invalid, the hospitals; develop intercessory prayer chain, provide special equipment for ministry to the blind, program for "adopting" elderly couples, transport the elderly to shop, etc., provide convalescent equipment, ministry to drug addicts, emergency food and clothing, etc.

Suggestive material is available for groups or individuals who wish to be stimulated by thought-provoking lists of service opportunities.[1] Let's face it. *The tasks are infinite . . . but God has a way of "nudging" you by his Spirit concerning the way to execute your gift.* And the point of all this is that each of us should seek God's guidance for the functions we are to perform.

Thus far I have stipulated various areas of supernatural *enablements* for service and various ways these gifts should then be *executed*. Now let us add that there are also various *effects* (results) which you can expect from the exercise of your gift.

Spiritual Gifts Result in a Variety of EFFECTS

In our key passage, verse 6 states, "and there are *diversities of operations*, but it is the same God who *worketh all in all*" (1 Cor. 12:6, key words italicized). This verse has been too casually rendered. Given closer scrutiny, it says something quite unique and wonderful. Let us more carefully examine verse 6.

What does "diversities of operations" mean? First, let me say it does *not* mean *a variety of gifts*, for that has already been said in verse 4. The word *operations* could better be translated manifestations, results, or effects. *This phrase speaks of a variety of supernatural "effects" which will result when you exercise your gift in service!*

Now direct your attention to the last part of the verse: "But it is the same God which worketh all in all." The word *worketh* is the participle form of the same Greek word *energeo*, which means *God-produced effects*. Thus, the Weymouth Translation renders it, "the same God who produces all the effects."

The phrase "all in all" means God will produce various kinds of effects (all) *in* everyone present (all). Therefore, the full meaning of this verse is: *Your gift will have a variety of effects, but it is God himself who produces all the effects in all who are present.*

Furthermore, the next verse, verse 7, goes on to say: "But the manifestation of the Spirit is given to every man to profit withal" (1 Cor. 12:7). This verse further reinforces the fact that *the effects of your gift can profit everyone present.*

Think with me through one more observation. Paul mentions the diversities of operations (effects) in verse 6. Then he supplies you with a list of them in verses 7-11. He mentions the diversities of operations, then immediately lists them in the following verses. That the list refers to various operations (effects) is more evident in the Greek. The word translated *working* in verse 10 is the same word translated *operations* (effects) in verse 6. And the word translated *worketh* in verse 11 is also the same word translated *operations* (effects) in verse 6. *So the author is still discussing operations (effects) through verse 11!* I repeat, verses 7-11 provide a list of the effects spoken of in verse 6. Verse 11 should be rendered: "All these *operates* that one and selfsame Spirit." This list refers to the various operations (effects) of your gift in the lives of those to whom you minister.

Paul, then, lists various effects—*but what I am getting at is these effects will not be evident in the person who is exercising the gift . . . but these effects will be evidenced in the lives of those to whom he ministers.*

One person in the audience might receive *a word of wisdom* (v. 8),
    another person might receive *a word of knowledge* (v. 8),
    another might receive added *faith* (v. 9),
    another some gift of *healing* (v. 9),
    another might receive some *miraculous* experience (v. 10),
    another might receive some *prophecy* (v. 10),
    another might be enabled to *discern a spirit* (v. 10),
    another might be moved to *ecstatic utterance* (v. 10).

There *will* be supernatural evidences . . . and the Holy Spirit produces as many of them as he chooses, in as many people as he chooses: "But all these results are brought about by one and the same spirit, allotting them to each individually as He pleases" (1 Cor. 12:11, Weymouth).

Obviously, this list was not meant to be in any way comprehensive. Seventeen pages could not list all the myriads of impressions and effects that could result from the exercise of a gift. These effects are samples; they represent specific types which will serve to validate your service as a proper exercise of a spiritual gift. *These effects are the signs which validate your gift, and it is in this sense that gifts are signs!*

We now see there are three aspects in the exercise of a spiritual gift: (1) Spiritual gifts are supernatural *enablings* in themselves. (2) They are variously *executed* as God leads you. (3) And the Holy Spirit will use their proper execution to produce various supernatural *effects* in others! *(Be sure you understand this!)*

The following columns list the areas of *enablement,* the means of *execution,* and the *effects* of spiritual gifts.

Enablements (Rom. 12:6-8)	Executions (1 Cor. 12:28)	Effects (1 Cor. 12:6-11)
1. Prophecy	1. Apostle	1. A word of wisdom
2. Ministry	2. Prophet	2. A word of knowledge
3. Teaching	3. Teacher	3. Faith
4. Exhorting	4. Evangelist	4. A gift of healing
5. Giving	5. Miracle Worker	5. A miracle
6. Ruling	6. Healing	6. A prophecy
7. Showing mercy	7. Helps	7. A discerning spirit
	8. Government	8. Diverse tongues
	9. Diversities of tongues	9. Interpretation of tongues

In all fairness, the above groupings represent a direct departure from the traditional interpretation. Most scholars list all the above twenty-five functions as basic spiritual gifts. In accordance with the terminology of this book, they would say they are all *enablements,* making no reference to any of them as either *executions* or *effects.* Therefore, in terms of our above groupings, the traditional interpretation would place all the functions in the *left* column and do away with the other two columns.

Actually, there are four places in the Bible where lists are provided with reference to spiritual gifts. Altogether, there are thirty functions listed in these four biblical passages. Traditionally, each function is considered a "gift." But *eleven* of them are mentioned more than once. Eliminating the duplications, there are about *nineteen* different "gift-functions" mentioned. *However, taking each of them as distinct and separate "gifts," there is almost total disagreement in terms of how to account for their varied characteristics.* Some seem permanent, while others are thought to have been temporary. Some are for speaking while others are for service. Scholars all recognize various similarities and dissimilarities, *but there is almost total disagreement on how to group them into categories.* One writer candidly admits that each biblical scholar will group the gifts differently. He lists seven separate groupings as examples and leaves you to choose one of the seven.[2] But it seems to me the Bible is more *precise* than that. As ingenious and generally helpful as such works are, I believe each has missed the essential key to a clear understanding of spiritual gifts by overlooking the significance of 1 Corinthians 12:4-6.

This key passage (1 Cor. 12:4-6) sets forth *three different aspects* with reference to a gift (enablements, executions, effects). And the different biblical lists exist for the precise purpose of setting forth these three aspects:

(1) The list of Romans 12:6-8 refers to the basic areas in which we are *enabled.*

(2) The list of 1 Corinthians 12:28-30 and the list of Ephesians 4:11 both refer to the way to *execute* your gift.

(3) The list of 1 Corinthians 12:8-10 refers to the *effects* of your gift in the life of others.

We have varied biblical lists, then, because there are three different aspects of a spiritual gift. Furthermore, while almost all of this book *will be relevant to one who holds to the more traditional viewpoint concerning the grouping of gifts,* I have ventured forth with this fresh approach with real confidence. I hold to this interpretation for several reasons . . . because of its biblical authenticity, its spiritual validity, its comparative simplicity, and its experiential reality. (Not that this interpretation is unique—Bill Gothard holds a very similar viewpoint.)

In conclusion, our three columns will be listed again. But this time we will underline the area of enablement, the manner of execution, and effects of a spiritual gift . . . in the experience of Billy Graham.

People all over the world are grateful that God gave Billy Graham the gift of *prophecy.* Out of the seven areas of enablement in Column A (below), we have set in bold type the gift God gave him. *However,* after having discovered the basic area of his enabling, then Dr. Graham had to determine how God would have him *execute* his gift in and through the church. (See second column below.)

(1) Note in Column B, God might have led Dr. Graham to exercise

his gift of prophecy as an *apostle* (missionary).

(2) Also note in Column B, God might well have led Dr. Graham to exercise his gift of prophecy as a *prophet* (pastor).

(3) Also note in Column B, God might have led Dr. Graham to exercise his gift of prophecy as a *teacher*.

(4) However, God led Dr. Graham to exercise his gift of prophecy as an evangelist (illustrated by the words *prophecy* and *evangelist* being in bold type in Columns A and B).

A. Enablements	B. Executions	C. Effects
(Rom. 12:6-8)	(1 Cor. 12:28)	(1 Cor. 12:6-11)
1. **Prophecy**	1. Apostle	1. **A word of wisdom**
2. Ministry	2. Prophet	2. **A word of knowledge**
3. Teaching	3. Teacher	3. **Faith**
4. Exhorting	4. **Evangelist**	4. A gift of healing
5. Giving	5. Miracle Worker	5. A miracle
6. Ruling	6. Healing	6. A prophecy
7. Showing mercy	7. Helps	7. A discerning spirit
	8. Government	8. Diverse tongues
	9. Diversities of tongues	9. Interpretation of tongues

Furthermore, after having determined the basic area of service in which he was *enabled* (from Column A) and the way in which he was to *execute* his gift (from Column B), Dr. Graham could then expect to see God produce certain *effects* as signs that he had truly discovered his gift (Column C). From *evangelist* in Column B, certain effects listed in Column C in the preceding illustration are in bold type to point out obvious results that do follow the exercise of Billy Graham's gift. For, when he preaches:

(1) Note in Column C, many receive *a word of wisdom* (they wise-up) about their need of salvation and make a "decision for Christ."

(2) Note in Column C, others receive *a word of knowledge* about *how* to become a Christian, thus make their "decision for Christ."

(3) Note in Column C, still others have their *faith* quickened to trust Christ for salvation, etc.

Various effects will result and all in response to God's use of Billy Graham's gift of prophecy.

Perhaps this will best illustrate the three different aspects of a spiritual gift. But, *again*, be sure you understand the three parts of a gift: (1) *Enablement*, the area in which you are gifted for service (12:4); (2) *Execution* (administration), the way in which your gift functions in and through the church (12:5); (3) *Effect* (operation), the results of your gift in other lives (12:6).

It is my deep and abiding conviction that God intends each and every Christian to be a faithful, fruitful servant. Furthermore, God has graced you with a spiritual gift for service which makes it *possible* for you to serve Him honorably and effectively. And God will hold you accountable as a *steward* for the development and deployment of your spiritual gift: "As every man hath received the gift, even so minister the same one to another, as good *stewards* of the manifold grace of God" (1 Pet. 4:10, italics added). And this is where the water hits the wheel in terms of mobilizing our full Christian work force. The key to productive Christian service is for each and every Christian to discover his spiritual gift for service, determine how God would have him *exercise* it, and verify it by its *effect* in the lives of others . . . as a part of God's redemptive purpose in this world!

Notes

1. The Southern Baptist Convention has published a *Project Guide* which provides endless suggestions (Brotherhood Commission, SBC, 1458 Poplar Ave., Memphis, Tenn. 38104).

2. Criswell, pp. 126-127.

8

The Guiding Light

Thus far I have emphasized the one great requirement for a God-guided life: how to *"present your bodies a living sacrifice"* (cross bearing). As suggested, this can best be done by denying yourself and committing your life to the Lord for all he wishes to do through you in service to others, as God's Spirit fills and uses you . . . especially along the line of activity in which he has spiritually gifted you. It works like this: To yield your life for God's use is to turn in a counter-direction, contrary to the flow of this self-centered world. And God will use the forces that work against you to: (1) shatter your self-sufficiency—and bring you to appropriate the filling (empowering) of God's Spirit; (2) keep you dependent upon your spiritual resources (Bible study, confession, prayer, worship, fellowship, and personal development); (3) at the same time use all your difficulties as a buffer . . . to smooth off the imperfections of your life, in his image; and (4) carry out his redemptive purposes through you.

All this is a *transforming process*, which is the second aspect mentioned in Romans 12:2 . . . the verse we have established as a New Testament "norm" for finding and following God's will: "And be not conformed to this world: but be ye transformed by the renewing of your mind, that ye may prove . . . the perfect will of God" (Rom. 12:2).

Now, think about this verse in terms of our illustration of an automobile which journeys through the night (chapter 2). For our world *is* in spiritual darkness . . . a "dominion of darkness" as Paul once put it (Col. 1:13, Amplified).

Fix your mind upon the image of that automobile as it travels through the dark . . . *with its headlights exposing the way.*

If you will excuse the play on words, the Holy Spirit provides two "head" lights to find and follow God's will for your life. These two "head" lights enable you to see the way of God in this world. Both of them are set forth in Romans 12:2.

"Head" Light No. 1: A Renewed Insight

Once again, note the second verse of our overall text. Paul urges: "And be not conformed to this world: but be ye transformed *by the renewing of your mind*, that ye may prove . . . [the] perfect will of God" (Rom. 12:2, italics added).

Now we come to grips with one of the most revealing terms of the Scriptures: *"By the renewing of your mind."* This is a weighty phrase, freighted with heavy significance. For "renewal of your mind" speaks of *the* process by which you discover God's will for your life. It is like a daybreak, by which God's will comes into view.

The word *mind* (*nous*) has reference to your basic insight into life. The Holy Spirit renews your mind in the sense that he changes your basic *insight*. So you may substitute for the term "renews your mind" a little more specific term, "renew your insight."

C. S. Lewis once told of standing in a dark toolshed. The sun was shining brightly outside. Through a cranny at the top of a door there came a brilliant sunbeam. Dr. Lewis said, "From where I stood that beam of light, with the specks of dust floating in it, was the most striking thing in the place." However, he was still looking only *at* the beam . . . not seeing things *by* it!

Suddenly Dr. Lewis moved so that the sunbeam fell on his eyes. And instantly the whole picture vanished. Now he saw no toolshed and no sunbeam. Instead, he was able to see through the crack of the slightly opened door and out into the brightly colorful world of floral paths and green shrubbery of the garden, outside the shed. Looking *at* a sunbeam and looking *through* the sunbeam are very different experiences. To look through a sunbeam at what it reveals . . . that is *insight*. That's the kind of light the Holy Spirit provides (John 16:13-15). And it was no less ponderous a thinker than philosopher Josiah Royce who once said: "Nowhere else is there a guide that can do more for you than to help quicken your insight." [1]

Now the question! *Just how does the Holy Spirit go about "renewing your mind (insight)" into life?*

In answer to that question, I would call your attention to J. B. Phillips and his brilliantly interpretive translation of Colossians 1:9. The verse speaks of "being filled with the knowledge of his will." However, in Phillips' translation, he rendered it: "That you may *see* things, as it were, *from his point of view* by being given *spiritual insight*." This is what it means to experience renewed insight. The Holy Spirit provides you with "spiritual insight" in terms of helping you see life from Christ's *point of view*. And a godly viewpoint is the one perspective from which you can discern the will of God for your life.

Now I realize that everyone has climbed up on the "soapbox" at one time or another to tell what is wrong with our world. But the one most sober, consistent observation the Bible makes is that unregenerate humanity views life from a wrong viewpoint, from a selfish perspective. That is why a renewed mind (insight) is so vital.

Man naturally sees life from a false point of view. He is basically selfish. Blinded by his hoggish desires, man lives only to please himself: "Those who let themselves be controlled by their lower natures live only to please themselves" (Rom. 8:5, TLB).

What's in it for me?—that is the viewpoint of unregenerate man.

In concentrated brevity, the Bible capsules the problem of man with a brief glimpse into the Garden of Eden . . . where man originally exercised his "free will" to choose against "God's will," so God gave man over to his own "self-will." And man has been stuck *with* himself (and stuck *on* himself) ever since. Archbishop William Temple stated it so concisely: "There is only one sin, and it is characteristic of the whole world. It is the self-will which prefers 'my' way to God's—which puts 'me' in the center where only God is in place." [2] Man is inherently selfish in all his activities.

Even as a Christian, how many hundreds of times I have recognized hidden motives behind my deeds. When I have done things "anonymously," it has often been motivated by a secret, inner expectation that God will bless me for it. At times I can fake it so brazenly, pretending such unselfish concern, as I help someone. But deep, deep, down inside, at the gut-level of my being, I sense the lurking ulterior motive, exposing my deed for the *selfish* act that it is.

In contrast to this blinding selfishness, recognize the pivotal significance of Paul's great prayer for a selfless, godly point of view: "We are asking God that you may see things, as it were, *from his point of view* by being given spiritual *insight and understanding*" (Col. 1:9, Phillips, italics added).

There you have one of the most vital truths in the Bible. The godly point of view, the viewpoint that transforms, is to see life from the standpoint of Jesus Christ. Paul speaks of Christians as having the "mind" of Christ (1 Cor. 2:16). Of course, this does not mean you have the *brains* of Christ. You have the living perspective of Christ. It means you can see life from the viewpoint of Christ. It is just such a perspective which the Holy Spirit provides: "Howbeit when he, the Spirit of truth, is come . . . he will not speak of himself . . he shall glorify me [Jesus]" (John 16:13-14).

Now let's drive down a stake and clearly establish our point. Our question is: How does the Holy Spirit go about renewing your mind or insight into life? The Spirit renews your basic insight into life by altering your *point of view*. You begin to see life from the perspective of Christ. But a further question surfaces at this point: What is the *method* by which the Holy Spirit alters your point of view? Perhaps without fully realizing it, we have established this already. You present your body "a living sacrifice" (Rom. 12:1), which is the same as saying you must deny yourself, take up your cross daily, and follow him (see Luke 9:23). *That is the process* by which God changes your point of view. Jesus said, "Take my yoke upon you, and learn of me" (Matt. 11:29). You learn of him as your life is yoked with his, in cross-bearing sacrifice for others. *The Holy Spirit uses this very activity to change the perspective of your life-center from self to the Savior.*

Furthermore, it is equally significant to establish the fact that this change of life-center *is* a process. It does not happen instantaneously. We are not talking about a one-time experience but a *"living* sacrifice," a steady, continual process.

Perhaps I can best explain the transforming effect of a renewed perspective by an example from another page of life. A favorite acquaintance of mine is the director of a drama department in a large high school. He is renowned for his ability to produce annual dramas of the highest excellence. Each year his plays draw large crowds. People come from miles away to enjoy an enchanted evening of theatrical delight. But it was only when he directed a play in which one of my daughters participated, *and I had occasion to attend some of the rehearsals,* that I discovered the secret of his success.

Apart from full backdrops and costumes, the rehearsals seemed just as unglamorous as you would expect . . . except for one thing. There was a remarkable sense of cohesion about everything that was done. Everyone on and off that stage seemed to be exclusively conscious of the director. Everything followed his bidding. It was as if a magic bond had been forged between him and each member of the cast. The play was put together very carefully, line upon line, scene upon scene. Again and again, lines and movements would be repeated before the director's all-seeing eyes. And he had the most effortless and winsome way of correcting each broken line and each awkward gesture. No one ever seemed to upstage another or steal a spotlight. For it was as if no one acted for himself, or to an imaginary audience, or even to each other. They were playing it all to the director, knowing he would commend or correct each person's performance. Endlessly, he would change and explain, encourage and instruct . . . until they could go through a scene without a word from him. For he became "internalized" by the cast. They came to act as if he were right there with them . . . at center stage. And you could recognize his mastery in them all!

So it is, when you live your life to the Savior, rather than "play it" to the galleries with the spotlight on yourself. You deny yourself and take up your cross by moving out into the world in a service relationship to others.

When you go to work, uppermost in your conscious thought throughout the day is how you can be a blessing to those around you . . . in terms of how well you do your work and in terms of those extra things you do as a help to others.

You recreate, do your grocery shopping, or engage in social activities, all with the same view in mind. As you do this *daily,* it becomes your life-style. Christ will be "internalized." The Holy Spirit will do a work in you and you will begin to see things from Christ's point of view.

Furthermore, the result of a renewed mind is a transformed outlook.

So a second "head" light is consequent to the first.

"Head" Light No. 2: A Changed Outlook

Now let us consider another aspect of the second verse in our overall text: "And be not conformed to this world: *but be ye transformed* by the renewing of your mind, that . . . ye might prove . . . the perfect will of God" (Rom. 12:2, italics added).

The word *transformed* is a rendering of the Greek verb *metamorphoō*. It is similar to our modern word, metamorphosis. This word speaks of a distinct, Spirit-produced change which results from the renewal of your mind, "transformed by the renewing of your mind." But *what* is changed?

It is generally assumed the verse has reference to the transformation of your "inner nature." And rightly so if you mean by "inner nature" the inward proclivities of a man which determine his responses to life. But in more common terms, it can simply be understood as a *change of your outlook on life.*

Let me elaborate. Each one of us has a *system of values* which determines our basic *outlook* on life. These values contain what we consider most important. All your habitual ways of acting rest on these values. For example: A person who places a high value on *prestigious position* in life might find this "value judgment" responsible for any number of decisions: (1) His choice of a prestigious car, (2) his membership in a prestigious "country club," (3) his affinity for prestigious clothes, (4) his drive toward prestigious vocational success, and (5) his willingness to head up some prestigious civic function.

However, our actions are most often a good deal more complicated because it is usually a combination of values which motivates a certain course of action. And many of our values are subconscious. Thus we are unaware of them.

One thing more about these values. Each of us will establish certain priorities within our value system (outlook on life). That is, we have a hierarchy of values, a rank or scale of importance. For example, a young athlete who values athletics and prizes a healthy body might still develop a harmful smoking habit when pressured by his *peer group* . . . if he values his peer group more than sports.

It is within your inner value system (outlook) that God's Spirit works his transformation of your life: The Holy Spirit "will convict and convince . . . about *sin* and about *righteousness* . . . and about *judgment*" (John 16:8, Amplified, italics added). That is: (1) about *wrong values* . . . "sin"; (2) About *right values* . . . "righteousness"; (3) About *eternal values* . . . "judgment to come"!

How do these values influence you? Psychologists explain the effects of your values in these terms: "Values provide a *perceptual grid* which gives a *selective orientation* to situations." Dr. Larry Richards gives this example: "Let's say that five people are standing on a street corner watching a smiling girl stride up the sidewalk. One is a dentist, one a hairdresser, one a dressmaker, one a coach, and one an optometrist. What does each see? Well, the dentist notices first her smile and white, even teeth. The hairdresser notices the way her hair is cut and shaped and if it fits her type of face. The first thing the dressmaker sees is the way her outfit is cut and trimmed. The coach notes her athletic swing and the way she carries her head and shoulders. And the optometrist, noting a slight squint, wonders if she has glasses and doesn't wear them because she thinks they might spoil her looks!" [3]

To each man one feature was more important and of more value to him (the perceptual grid) than other features, so he naturally looked first of all (selective orientation) at that which was most important to him. We operate that way all the time.

Our values filter out what is *un*important to us and focus our attention on what is important to us. They determine our outlook! And our outlook is *crucial* in determining all the decisions we make in life, the type of person we become, and the kind of life we choose to lead. This is the meaning of the verse which says that as a man "thinketh in his heart, so is he" (Prov. 23:7).

So, what has all this to do with finding God's will for your life? Everything!

To develop a godly value system is to gain a godly outlook on life. You will be able to detect God's will by the very nature of the fact that you will begin to see life as he sees it. That is exactly what David had in mind: "I will instruct thee and teach thee in the way which thou shalt go: I will guide thee with mine eye" (Ps. 32:8).

This verse not only sets forth a *promise* of guidance—"I will instruct thee and teach thee in the way thou shalt go"—it also sets forth God's *procedure* of guidance—"I will guide thee with mine eye." For a long time I wondered what God meant by the procedure—"I will guide thee with mine eye." Finally, the meaning dawned on me. Through a new value system *you gain a godly "outlook" on life . . . that is, you begin to see things as God sees them.* It will be as if he guides you with his eye in that he enables you to see *through* his eyes!

The New Testament verifies it. God wishes to reveal his will by the process of giving you his insight: "Make you perfect in every good work to do his will, *working in you* that which is well pleasing *in his sight*" (Heb. 13:21, italics added).

To determine God's will about most things, you must experience what Paul prayed for (as mentioned earlier): "We are asking God that you may see things, as it were, from his point of view by being given spiritual insight and understanding . . . that your outward lives may bring credit to your master's name. . . . (Col. 1:9-10, Phillips)

Do not miss the meaning of what I am saying. I am not suggesting a natural psychological process that will occur inside a person apart from the work of God. Although this process can be understood psychologically, the dynamic for it comes from the Holy Spirit. This is a God-wrought phenomena that would never come off except the Holy Spirit quickens the inner psychological process of the Christian's life to accomplish what would be inexplicable apart from him. God changes us. At the very core of our being, he alters our system of values in such a transforming way that we begin to see through his eyes. If a person doesn't wake up in a brand-new world and *begin* to see things differently after a professed salvation experience, it is quite doubtful that he has encountered God in a saving way. And if any so-called *deeper* experience with God fails to open your eyes wider, then all you have experienced is a temporary emotional uplift. God changes your outlook on life. And in so doing, he influences every decision you make.

All this should teach us at least two very important lessons. First, God's will must be *intensely appropriated.*

To find God's will is no *easy* task. It necessitates a sustained life-style of cross-bearing commitment through which God breaks through to displace your natural selfishness with a new viewpoint on life. You gain a Christ-centered viewpoint which will, in turn, alter your basic system of values and change your outlook to the point that you begin to see life as God sees it. Such an outlook comes progressively, but gradually . . . over the years. It requires an *intense* commitment of your life.

To the contrary, when most Christians ask the question—"How can I know God's will for my life?"—*what they really want is a thirty-minute formula!* Again and again I have counseled with someone who has sought me out for help in determining God's will about a matter. They wanted an immediate solution. But they were in no condition to determine God's will. They lacked the perspective to see it. They were obsessed with their own wishes. They had to be led back onto the main road of sacrificial living. Only by the process of repentance and obedience could they regain the insight and outlook necessary to determine God's will.

God's will must never be thought of as an *objective plan.* What you are seeking is the will of another *person*—a person for whom you are to have such love that you seek to know him—and seek to know him well enough to anticipate his wishes. This takes time and experience!

For example, as an itinerant conference speaker, I spent my first three years exclusively teaching in the Richard Hogue evangelistic crusades. I recall a citywide crusade in which I was meeting with a group of local pastors just prior to the evening service. Our conversation concerned an extremely complicated matter of utmost significance to the crusade. A decision had to be rendered immediately . . . and Richard was running late to the services because of a dinner engagement. The pastors were quite hesitant about making any decision without discussing it with Richard. So they turned to me. And I immediately told them what Richard would want done.

Then, very naturally, a pastor asked, "Are you sure you know Richard's mind on this matter?"

I replied without the slightest hesitation, "Yes, I know this is exactly what he would have you do."

It was only later that I reflected back upon the incident and realized its significance. *I had grown to know a man so well that I could tell you his will about certain matters.* I knew how he would see it. Furthermore, I had been *certain*. But such knowledge was not quickly gained. I had spent week after week with him for several years. There were countless late-night talk sessions and endless hours of prayer and counsel. On top of this add weeks of co-labor in the closest kind of comradeship . . . *then I could see through his eyes!*

However, for those who do seek God's will intensely, as the preceding illustration bears out: Much of God's will can then be *instantly appropriated*. When a serious consideration is given to doing God's will, one of the first discoveries you make is that about 90 percent of your decisions must be made without significant time in which to weigh your action.

Most decisions must be made quickly in the course of your daily round of activities. That's the way life is. There is no time for prolonged consideration. So the only way to do God's will in most matters is for his wishes to become "second nature" to you.

Here is the way to do it: (1) Zero in on Jesus at the beginning of each morning. That is, take time to fix your mind on him. Praise him for yesterday's guidance. Tell him you want to follow his wishes again today and ask for his guidance: "Cause me to hear thy lovingkindness in the morning . . . cause me to know thy way wherein I should walk; for I lift my soul up to thee" (Ps. 143:8).

(2) The next step is to "deny yourself . . . daily" (Luke 9:23). Make it your practice to think through your anticipated schedule for that day. Deny yourself with regard to that day's schedule. That is, examine your heart with that day's activities in mind, and be certain you are *willing* to do what God wants. Be painstaking and transparently honest, for, "The heart is the most deceitful thing there is" (Jer. 17:9, TLB).

Are you willing to do God's will? This is the crucial question. Be careful not to pray like the young fellow about his sweetheart: "God, I want to do your will in every area of my life . . . but, please, you *must* give me Mary Lou."

Almost daily I examine myself and find subconscious resistance toward one kind of duty or another. But when I consciously confront myself about this rebellion, admit (confess) it, and really decide to do the will of God, I usually follow through in effortless obedience.

But it takes a *daily* self-denial. Jesus said, "Deny yourself . . . daily" (Luke 9:23). Paul said, "I die daily" (1 Cor. 15:31). A steadfast faithfulness to daily deny your own self-will is the basic requirement for finding and following the will of God. Also, deny your own self-will and choose the Lord's will in advance for the situations you have not anticipated during the day. Do this by faith.

(3) Depart to "practice his presence." Live that day by him and *for* him . . . being sure "all that thrills your soul is Jesus!"

(4) Don't forget to practice "thought prayer." That is, learn to aim a thought heavenward as a means of prayer. At the very instant you contemplate each and every decision, though it be but a moment, acknowledge your need and claim the mind of Christ. Follow the example of Nehemiah. When the king turned to Nehemiah and he had that momentary opportunity to make his request, Nehemiah wrote: "*I prayed to the God of heaven. And I said unto the king*" (Neh. 2:4-5, italics added). Now I hardly see Nehemiah saying to the king: "Stand aside a moment, will you, king, and hold my things while I kneel down here. I want to pray about this matter for a few minutes. So stand there quietly while I do so, then I have a request to make of you."

No, Nehemiah prayed a "thought prayer." Even as he lifted his eyes to meet the gaze of the king, he whispered a prayer "under his breath," so to speak. In the wink of an eye he thoughtfully acknowledged his need and claimed God's guidance, then made his request to the king. God knows that this method of acknowledgement keeps you in constant dependence upon him: "Trust in the Lord. . . . *in all thy ways acknowledge him* and he shall direct thy paths" (Prov. 3:5-6, italics added).

(5) Then follow your "head" lights. Boldly trust God for his insight and outlook. Make your decisions on the basis of your lights *"from within."* Be positive. Never waiver. Confidently decide!

(6) Then follow through and do God's will . . . once you know it.

(7) Do it all for the fullest expression of his life through yours, as a witness to our lost and straying world. Then you will understand why J. Sidlow Baxter would write: "One of the most elevating of all experiences on this earth is to go through one's days and hours with

an unbroken awareness of Godguidedness." [4]

Notes

1. Josiah Royce, *The Religious Aspects of Philosophy* (New York: Harper and Brothers, 1958), p. 470.

2. William Temple, *Readings in St. John's Gospel* (London: Macmillan Co., 1963), p. 24.

3. Larry Richards, *What's In It for Me?* (Chicago: Moody Press, 1970), pp. 62-63.

4. J. Sidlow Baxter, *His Deeper Work in Us* (London: Marshall, Morgan, and Scott, 1967), p. 159.

9

The Second Look

To find and follow God's will for your life, you must first learn to look *from within*. This was the emphasis of our previous chapter. You must depend on your "head" lights. Take advantage of the "insight" and "outlook" God has already given you. Choose God's will in advance, at the beginning of your day. Then depend on your light "from within" . . . trusting God to help you see each situation through his eyes.

This might be more than you can say grace over . . . at first. It takes some getting used to. If plagued with a Timothy Temperament (low self-esteem), you could get rather "nervous" about assuming such an ability, especially with regard to your major decisions.

However, there is another step to be taken in determining God's will for your life. But this step is conditional. That is, it is limited to occasions when you have time to contemplate your decision and look at all sides of a matter. And this is often the case with major decisions.

Inherent in our overall text is instruction for a *second look*. Indeed, all the previous suggestions of our text lead up to the last phrase . . . and the last phrase should be seen over against and in apposition to the previous ones: "That ye may prove what is that good and acceptable, and perfect will of God" (Rom. 12:2). But what does it mean "to *prove* . . . the will of God"? The original word here translated *prove* is *dokimazo*, elsewhere translated *trial* (Jas. 1:3). To "prove" the will of God means you *test* it!

First you look "from within" for guidance. Then take a second look. Test what you have seen. Sometimes this testing is but the mental reflection of a few moments. But as time allows it, take a *second look*. I know a lot of folks who fell in love at "first sight" . . . but now wish they had taken a second look!

The study of divine guidance, in itself, is one of the deepest truths the mind of man can fathom. Such a study necessitates your understanding and acceptance of God's "Divine Superintending Providence." This is the doctrinal promise upon which all faith in guidance rests. This great doctrine declares that God has ultimate control over this world. He is sovereign in every single thing that happens in it. And you are no exception, for God supernaturally governs all that goes on around *you* in order to reveal and realize his will in your experience. God is always there before you. He can alter the events which surround you. He remains available to you—so that you can actually test and prove his will. Your part is to scan the horizon of God's providence and read the outward signs which God arranges, in order to prove or verify your "inward" impressions.

God's providential guidance . . . and your test of it . . . are God's "fail-safe" precautions to insure a clear communication of his will.

One of the reasons you can trust your light "from within" and your ability to discern God's will is because God has provided these additional outward signs to guide you. These road guides either confirm or contradict your inward sense of direction.

Your Road Map—the Scriptures

You should never accept as divine guidance any course of action which is contrary to the Scriptures. This is the first rule of guidance. Your map is the Bible. Follow it. For example, you can be certain God will never lead you in a course of action which has been decided in a state of rage. Such an action *is* contrary to the Scriptures: "For the wrath of man worketh not the righteousness of God" (Jas. 1:20). That was the mistake of the elder brother in the parable of the prodigal son: "He was angry, and would not go in" (Luke 15:28). The Scriptures veto any impression which arises in wrath.

Furthermore, your personal insight must not only bow to specific scriptural contradiction but also to the *principles* and *the very sense* of Scripture. For example, consider the actual wording in the verse which says, "Be ye not unequally yoked together with unbelievers" (2 Cor. 6:14). Actually, this statement was *not* made in reference to marriage. But it is directly applicable, in principle. And if it finds an aspiring Christian preparing to marry a non-Christian, it should stop them "dead in their tracks!"

As you begin to gain a deeper spiritual understanding of God's perfect will, it is important to remember that isolated texts often tend to be carried too far. An isolated text can be made to sanction that which the principles of the Bible disallow. Hannah Whitall Smith believed that all fanaticism comes in this way.[1]

For example, one isolated text which is easily abused is found in James 5:16. "Confess your faults one to another." Occasionally I find this verse used to the extreme, as if Christians are to stand up among other Christians and confess everything and anything to everyone and anyone. However, there are biblical principles which limit the act of confession. (1) You are not to confess just *everything* because of the biblical principle which forbids sordid conversation: "It is a shame even to speak of those things which are done of them in secret" (Eph. 5:12). (2) You are not to confess just *anything* because of the principle against sharing knowledge in such a way that it "degenerates into gossip" (1 Tim. 5:13, Phillips). If sins are freely confessed in the presence of uninvolved parties, it can become gossip. (3) You do not always confess before *everyone* because of a biblical precedent against hanging your dirty laundry out in public. "And the seed of Israel separated themselves from *all strangers*, and stood and confessed their sins" (Neh. 9:2, italics added). (4) You don't run out rashly to confess just any sin to *anyone* because, in principle, confession is to heal broken relationships, not open new wounds: "There are those who speak rashly like the piercing of a sword, but the tongue of the wise brings healing" (Prov. 12:18, Amplified). Never cleanse your conscience with someone else's tears!

As time allows it, always take a second look to test your impressions by God's word. God will never lead you contrary to the Scriptures.

But there are other signals by which God will confirm or contradict your inner conviction.

Your Red Lights—the Character of God

God is "light" (1 John 1:5). This means the character of God "makes it possible to see." In the light of God's character you can evaluate your way of life for what it is. Furthermore, God's character never changes: "the source of all Light. In Him there is no variation, nor the shadow of change" (Jas. 1:17, Weymouth). Since God never changes, you can be certain he will never lead you to do anything "out of character" with himself. Therefore, *you should never accept as divine guidance any course of action contrary to the character of God.*

1. Test your leading against the character of God's *ways.* For example, not long ago I was a pulpit guest of a church in Alabama. The pastor of the church suffers from an occupational hazard which is characteristic of the ministry: He is as busy as a one-armed paper hanger.

But busy as he is, his natural warmth and genuine expressiveness has helped him maintain solid personal relationships with both his parishioners and his family. In fact, the pastor's son not only has real, heartfelt love and appreciation for his dad but a great deal of understanding about the burden of his father's rigid work schedule . . . so much so that the boy decided on quite a sacrificial plan as a means of encouragement for his father. And a few days later, on the morning of his dad's birthday, the son greeted him at the breakfast table with the news, "Dad, you have worked so hard lately that I have decided for your birthday *I will play with you all day long!*"

Now this dad was far too tender to risk his boy's thinking he might not *want* to play little boys' games all day long, so they wrestled and climbed, played Monopoly, then basketball, skated, played marbles, and finished the day off with a softball game. The pastor was still hobbling around when I arrived for my conference!

This made me wonder: Is *our* heavenly Father *really* interested in our taking his day up with those long, verbose, endless prayers? The character of our *gracious God* tells me prayer is not overcoming God's reluctance but accepting his willingness.

I wonder, too, if God really wants to spend his day with us running to and fro at ninety-miles-an-hour as if he desperately needs our help in every function of the church. The character of our *all-sufficient God* tells me he is not nearly as interested in what we can do for him as what he can do through us (which requires *some* time for making ourselves usable).

I also wonder if God really enjoys our taking his day up by making a game out of our spiritual relationship, as if everything has to be light, tranquil, and gay. The character of our *wrathful God* tells me there is also a deathly urgency about our ministry!

God's character can function as a red light to stop us when our thinking goes wrong. Many times God's great men of Scripture altered a certain course of action with no more verification for their decision than the character of God. The ageless question of the state of the heathen in the day of judgment seemed to be answered for Abraham by his certainty of the *righteousness of God*. When prayerfully interceding with regard to the judgment of Sodom, he said, "Shall not the Judge of all the earth do *right?*" (Gen. 18:25, italics added). I believe this is yet the ultimate answer for those who ask about the state of the heathen in the day of God's judgment.

These are but a few examples of the manner in which you can test your inner spiritual impression against the character of God. Any time you feel led in a direction which is contrary with God's ways, consider this a red light . . . stop and wait for further guidance!

2. Test your leading against the character of God's *wisdom*. The epistle of James sets forth a *compendium* on the changeless character of godly wisdom: "But the wisdom that is from above is first pure, then peaceable, gentle, and easy to be entreated, full of mercy and good fruits, without partiality, and without hypocrisy" (Jas. 3:17).

Let us examine each characteristic mentioned in this verse and see how it can contradict an inward sense of direction . . . thus serve as a "red light," causing you to stop and wait for further guidance.

Godly wisdom is *pure*. This biblical word "pure" means *single-mindedness*. In the next chapter James says "purify your hearts, ye double minded" (Jas. 4:8). Godly wisdom is decisive. It never marches to a dozen different drums. It never wavers. It knows its own mind. It is stable, while "a double minded man is unstable in all his ways" (Jas. 1:8). Do you vacillate between two decisions? Are you wavering in your conclusions? If so, consider this a *red light!* Stop and wait for further guidance.

Godly wisdom is *peaceable*. The Greek word for peace here is derived from the root *eirenē*. When it is used of men, its basic meaning is right relationships between man and man, and between man and God. The context of this verse indicates the former; *eirenē* refers here to relationship between man and man. For the preceding verse speaks out against envy and strife between men (Jas. 3:16) . . . and the following verse speaks of making peace between men (3:18). Is your intended course of action divisive? Will it cause strife between men? If so, there must be another way to go . . . consider this a *red light!*

I know of a pastor and an associate pastor who both seriously considered resigning their church positions because of differences between them. However, each decided against resigning because such a course of action by either of them *would have caused division in the church.* Instead, they sought reconciliation . . . and God delightfully blessed their decision.

Godly wisdom is *gentle.* If God gives you wisdom, it will come as a *gentle nudge.* God is never pushy. He always gives you unhurried guidance. A young minister's wife asked my opinion about an impression to quit her job. I doubted her intended decision because she felt urged upon to make a prayerless, rushed decision. God leads by a gentle nudge. Do you feel the urge to make a hurried decision? Is there vivid emotion and nervous apprehension about this decision? Is this an impulsive decision? Have you been unwilling to stop and pray about it? Are you being pushed? If so, consider this a *red light!* Stop and wait for further guidance.

God's wisdom is *easy to be entreated.* Godly wisdom is never unreasonably rigid. It is attained by those who are objective and approachable. Are you dogmatically or fanatically isolated in your decision? Among those truly spiritual, are you the only one who thinks that way? Are you unapproachable in that it makes you nervous or irritable when people question your reasoning? If so, consider this a *red light!*

God's wisdom is *full of mercy and good fruits.* God leads people to merciful action. The fruit of his activity is always good. Is your intended course of action less than the merciful thing to do? Will it lead you into an activity which is less than morally uplifting? Is your decision one of pure self-interest? Will the consequences (fruits) of your actions be harmful? If so, consider this a *red light!*

Godly wisdom is *impartial.* Godly wisdom is thoroughly open-minded and objective. Godly decisions are made without prejudgment. Has your sense of leading been influenced by preconceived ideas? Is your decision prejudiced or bigoted? Is it influenced by sectarianism or undue bias? Is it narrowminded, unfair, or intolerant? Is it provincial? If so, consider this a *red light!*

Godly wisdom is without *hypocrisy.* Godly wisdom is honest. It has nothing to hide. Such integrity is an absolute necessity for God's guidance: "The integrity of the upright shall guide them" (Prov. 11:3).

Are you hesitant about thoroughly examining your reasons for a decision? Are you defensive? Are you slow to distrust yourself? Does your lack of self-reflection reveal an ulterior motive behind your intended course of action? If so, consider this a *red light!*

As time allows it, you should check every impression "from within" against the character of God's ways and wisdom. When you are impressed about a course of action and it is commensurate with the changeless character of God, this should serve as a *green light* . . . as additional verification. Press on unless God provides some other sign to alter your course. If, on the other hand, your inward impression is contrary to the character of God, this should serve as a *red light.* Stop for further guidance!

Road Signs . . . Your Circumstances

God can also use all manner of circumstances as signs to guide you along the way. He will often devise some obvious and timely turn of events to verify his will. With uncanny timing, you will experience the arrival of a bit of news, some inexplicable happening, some unanticipated problem, or some unique incident . . . some kind of an additional factor will fall into place and help you determine God's will.

Therefore, when you have time to take a "second look" . . . it is wise to check your road signs, the circumstantial providences by which God verifies his will.

Sometimes these circumstances will be dramatic . . . almost overwhelming. For example, several years ago a close friend, John LaNoue, came to a "crossroad" in his life. At that time he was serving on the staff of the Texas Baptist Convention. He had just received an invitation to head up a laymen-oriented missionary program called "Amigos Internationalis." Simultaneously, he was being sought for a position with the Sunday School Board. John was faced with a decision. Was it God's will for him to (1) remain in his present position, (2) head up "Amigos Internationalis," or (3) accept the Sunday School Board position? It was a difficult decision.

After several weeks of consideration, John found himself unable to discover God's will. He was impressed that God seemed to be leading toward a vocational change, but he vacillated between an inward urge to go with "Amigos Internationalis" and an occasional nudge to accept the Sunday School Board position. However, the latter consideration was clouded by *fear*. The Board is located in Nashville, Tennessee . . . the worst possible place for his son's hypersensitive allergic condition. He would not be able to afford a satisfactory home in the Nashville area. And he feared the drastic change of ministry involved in the Sunday School Board position.

It was at this time that Dr. James Croft took John and his wife to a special "prayer and praise" service in an Episcopal church. The week-night service was a highly inspirational hour. The people present shared their recent experiences with Christ, praised God for each account of his sustaining care, then spent time in intercessory prayer. Just before the service closed, a strange thing took place. A man stood to say, "God has given me a word concerning someone here, and I must share it. The message is: 'Come and follow me, my little children; stay close to my body; I will take care of you; you need have no *fear.*'" John immediately turned to speak to his wife, but she took the words right out of his mouth. "This message was for us," she said. And they wrote it down.

Speaking about it later that night, they began to ask themselves, "Is God telling us our fears of Nashville are ungrounded?"

It was the very next day that a medical doctor and his wife, Dr. and Mrs. Lamar McNew, dropped by the LaNoue home for a visit. They had come to encourage John about accepting the "Amigos Internationalis" position. John said nothing about the night before but simply said he was not fully certain.

But before leaving, Dr. McNew said, "John, let's just pray right now and ask God to reveal something more definite about this matter." Both men and their wives knelt to pray. And it was during their prayer time that Mrs. McNew began sobbing audibly, then spoke: "I have never done this before, but I have the strongest impression from God and I must share it." Her exact words were: "Come and follow me, my little children; stay close to my body; I will take care of you; you need have no *fear*." Furthermore, without informing the McNews this was precisely the same message as the night before, each one wrote on a note of paper what they felt to be God's will. Amazingly, (though all four actually desired that the choice be "Amigos Internationalis) each of them wrote: *"The Sunday School Board."*

Needless to say, John accepted the position with the Sunday School Board. All John's fears were unfounded. God has taken care of his son's health problem. He provided an even larger home than they had before and blessed John in his new area of ministry!

Nor should we ever be so foolish as to "write off" such circumstances as purely coincidental. J. Sidlow Baxter is incisively correct in his reasons why it would be *un*scientific to dismiss them as mere coincidence:

> First they reveal *purpose*, whereas coincidence is blindly fortuitous. Second, they express *coherence*, especially those which form a *chain* of guidance, link by link, whereas mere coincidence is patternless chance. Third, they are such direct answers to prayer, in many cases, as to establish a cause-and-effect relation, whereas coincidence is a quite mindless turn of circumstances which cannot have *any* such connection.[2]

However, let me be quick to say that circumstantial signs need not be extraordinary events of abnormal means. They need not strike from out of nowhere like a bolt of lightning. The simplest incident, when perfectly timed, can illicit the most certain response from those who are spiritually sensitive.

I once found myself torn between two coveted opportunities of service. I felt more led to one of the two but needed a final confirmation. And I got it. One night I received two telephone calls in which both opportunities were offered. But the calls came twenty minutes apart. I made my decision with great confidence because the call about the situation to which I already felt impressed came *twenty minutes earlier*. On the basis of that, I considered it a confirmation of my call coming first, leading to a decision that has proven sound. Sometimes the final piece of a puzzle falls in terms of the slightest thing, like a twenty-minute difference in the time of a telephone call. But it is so timely that God uses it to verify a sense of direction . . . and deep down it strengthens your conviction about a course of action.

But rarely ever would you make a decision concerning God's will for your life on the basis of circumstances *alone*. Indeed, it is worth a moment's reflection to refer back to our illustration about John LaNoue's vocational decision. Even after John had received something as seemingly providential as two identical messages from quite separate sources, he still considered these circumstances only corroborative. He sought a *final* answer through earnest prayer.

Circumstances themselves are untrustworthy. They are fickle. They fluctuate. Their signs are so temporary that if they say "Good morning," you had better call the weather bureau and make sure.

Lin Yutang, a Chinese philosopher, tells of an ancient Oriental parable that points out how temporary and impermanent circumstance can be. "An old man lived with his son in an abandoned fort. One night the old man's horse—the only horse he had—wandered away, and his neighbors all came to say how sorry they were about his misfortune. He said, 'How do you know this is *ill* fortune?' A week later the horse came home, bringing with him a whole herd of wild horses. The neighbors came again, helped him capture the wild horses, and congratulated him on his good fortune. The old man smiled and asked, 'How do you know this is *good* fortune?' As the days went on, the old man's son took to riding the horses; one day he was thrown and wound up with a crippled leg. The neighbors appeared again, like a Greek chorus, to tell him how sorry they were about his bad luck, but the old man asked, 'How do you know it is *bad* luck?' In less than a week, along came a Chinese war Lord conscripting all able-bodied men for his private little war, but the old man's son, being a cripple, missed the draft. Once more came the neighbors to rejoice with him in his good luck, and once more the old man said, 'How do you know this is *good* luck?' The story ends there although it could go on forever." [3]

Circumstances alone are inconclusive evidence. They can change sides faster than a windshield wiper. They lack finality. However, God is in sovereign control of this world. Sometimes he takes circumstances in hand. He uniquely *times* them. Their effect will be much like that of the last piece of a jigsaw puzzle which fits right into place. Such circumstances can be a marvelous corroborative evidence of God's will in a matter.

Your Compass . . . Conscience

One of the most accurate instruments for testing your light "from within," concerning an intended course of action, is a type of built-in compass in the human spirit . . . your conscience. Your conscience is a God-given instrument for self-judgment. You are to test a course of action in the light of its pronouncements: "their conscience also bearing witness, and their thoughts the mean while accusing or excusing one another" (Rom. 2:15). Your conscience bears witness on the basis of what is morally right. It brings to your decision-making process a sense of "ought"—"what you ought to do"!

However, your first duty is not to *follow* conscience but to *enlighten* it. Conscience is not the law book in the courtroom. It is the judge. And the decisions of a judge are only as good as the law by which he judges. Give your conscience right values by which to judge, and its decisions will be uniform, absolute (infallible), and authoritative. Properly magnetized, a compass is an unerring judge of direction. It always points the right way. Properly edified, your conscience is also an unerring judge of direction . . . it always points the right way.

Incidentally, once you begin your "Journey into Usefulness," as we have said, the Lord will enable you to see life from his point of view . . . and you will begin to assimilate his values. These very values form the basis of judgment (law) by which your conscience can become a critical instrument for testing your light "from within." Inasmuch as time allows it, you should submit every contemplated course of action to the careful scrutiny of a sensitive conscience. Ask yourself, "Is this what I ought to do?"

The indicator of your compass called conscience is a *peaceful state of mind*. This is the way your conscience registers its sense of "ought-ness" within you. When a contemplated action is *contrary* to your set of godly values, the conscience will disturb your peaceful state of mind. On the other hand, when a course of action *corresponds* with your set of godly values, the conscience strengthens your peaceful state. That is why the Bible says that peace should *rule* in your hearts: "And let the peace . . . rule (act as umpire continually) in your hearts—*deciding and settling with finality all questions that arise in your minds—[in that peaceful state]*" (Col. 3:15, Amplified, italics added).

The principle, then, *is to refuse any "supposed" guidance which disturbs your inner sense of peace.* Seldom, if ever, will God expect you to make a decision before you get his peace about a matter. The peace of God is a garrison to guard your hearts and minds against wrong (see Phil. 4:7). Never make a decision when you are "all worked up" inside. Someone rightly said that turmoil is like the tinfoil dropped by enemy planes—it jams your spiritual radar.

Jesus once caused a group of men to examine a matter in the light of their consciences. It resulted in a dynamic turn of events. A group of Pharisees "brought unto him a woman taken in adultery" (John 8:3). Dragging her through the crowd, the hooting band of Pharisees gathered around Jesus and threw the woman into the dust at his feet. With rocks in hand, they had every intention of stoning the woman. But first they questioned Jesus about his will in the matter: "What sayest thou?" (8:5).

Jesus answered their question with a dramatic gesture. He "stooped down, and with his finger wrote on the ground" (8:6). This is the only time the Bible ever says Jesus wrote anything. And it has always been my impression that he stooped down and wrote out the secret sins of each accuser in the circle . . . over against his feet. Then Jesus stood up and said, "He that is without sin among you, let him first cast a stone at her" (8:7). And the accusers, *"being convicted by their own conscience,"* dropped their stones one by one and turned to walk away.

Jesus provided a new perspective: Only the innocent may condemn. Based upon that law, their conscience convicted them that their intended course of action was wrong. And your conscience will often do the same for you!

One of the most neglected, yet vital and practical, steps to take in order to find and follow the will of God for your life is to *develop a good conscience.*

But do not be mistaken at this point. For years I thought a "good" conscience was an *untroubled* one. Not necessarily! Acting against the dictates of your conscience will weaken, even defile it: "And their conscience being weak is defiled" (1 Cor. 8:7). The hypocrite who *consciously* lives a lie—his conscience might be so defiled that it is untroubled because it is "as dead as seared flesh" (1 Tim. 4:2, Phillips).

Quite to the contrary, a "good" conscience is one that has the *capacity* to "trouble" your mind. Some guilt-pangs are as painful as splinters in the quick . . . so that you will change a course of action rather than persist in the wrong direction.

A good conscience is an *honest* one: "For we trust we have a good conscience, in all things willing to live honestly" (Heb. 13:18). The more painstakingly and explicitly you obey your conscience, the most exacting are its judgments. A good conscience is so honest and sensitive that it will react to the slightest veering away from your values. For example, a minister or evangelist with a good conscience will be so honest he will feel guilty about saying there were fourteen decisions in a service when, in fact, there were only twelve! A housewife with a good conscience will immediately return the excess money to a cashier who mistakenly gave her too much change. And a businessman with an honest conscience would have some qualms about even driving over the speed limit on his way to work.

Like a rare flower, a good conscience deserves delicate cultivation. It grows in a rare atmosphere. For such a conscience is usually developed through the earnest and habitual self-scrutiny of your *confession* time . . . alone, in your "closet" of prayer.

A good conscience can be a powerful asset in determining God's will. It helps you test the moral rightness of a course of action . . . it tells you what you *ought* to do. Check your sense of direction by it like a traveler refers to his compass.

In summary, when you take that second look to test an intended course of action, God uses four road guides to confirm or contradict your inward impression: (1) Check your road map . . . *the Scriptures.* (2) Check your red lights . . . *the character of God.* (3) Check your road signs . . . *circumstances.* (4) Check your compass . . . *conscience.*

But the real genius of this approach is that you do not make a decision except when absolutely necessary unless all (I repeat, *all*) four of your outward signs verify your light "from within." Always try to continue on your present course until you can test a new sense of direction to be sure the Scriptures, the character of God's ways and wisdom, circumstances, and your conscience all concur with your inward impression. You want all four to harmonize *before* you accept a leading as God's will. Don't make a decision on the strength of a confirmation in two or three of these areas. When possible, wait in prayer until all four of them harmonize with your "inner leading." Then act!

In the back of this book you will find a guide sheet which summarizes all these various road-signs . . . *and the following examples will illustrate how I have used it.*

I received a telephone call from the minister of music of a church in upper Wyoming. I was once his pastor. But now he is a full-time minister of music and it seems he influenced his pastor to invite my family to their church for a conference on spiritual renewal.

After seeking an "inner leading" in the manner in which I have suggested, I felt very uncertain about the matter, but finally "came up" with an impression to accept their invitation. Then I followed-through to take a "second look" and confirm my "inner leading." To do so I drew a line down the center of a blank piece of paper. The left side I labeled *Contradictions*, and the right side I labeled *"Final Thoughts."*

I placed my blank sheet of paper *alongside* a guide sheet (like the one at the back of this book) and began to ask myself the second battery of questions in order to test my leading. However, as I examined the invitation in the light of these questions I discovered several matters which seemed to contradict my initial impression. On the next page is a copy of the *lower-half* of the guide sheet which also shows my blank sheet of paper to the side . . . and my responses recorded on it.

Examine it and look under the column heading which says: *"Contradictions."* Looking down the column you will see the questions stimulated about five contradictions to my "initial leading." *These five negative reactions were all I had on the sheet of paper at first.*

However, I prayerfully meditated over the sheet for the next few days and, one by one, God began to give me a reassuring confirmation to offset each contradiction. Look at the illustration again and glance down the column to the right . . . labeled "Final Thoughts." There you will see the thoughts that, to my mind, minimized or eliminated each contradiction . . . and confirmed my "inner leading" to accept the invitation to Wyoming. Now I had an "inner leading" which was verified by Scriptures, the character of God, circumstances, and conscience. (Think with me! If the *contradictions* had remained . . . I would have felt my "inner leading" was wrong.)

We went. The meeting was fabulous and the love offering for our family was much more than adequate. But that is not all. A wonderful lady in that church was led of God to *give* us a bus for our travels. The bus had been converted into a motor home. We kept it almost two years, then gave it to another Christian worker who could use it more effectively, in exchange for *his* motor home. Then we sold his unit for the down payment of our present homestead . . . and the bus is still being used in God's work!

Only heaven will reveal the many marvelous blessings we all have missed because of our failure to seriously and carefully seek God's will. Be spontaneous and confident to claim God's mind in the case of instantaneous decisions. To the contrary, be cautious and deliberate when you have time to take a *second look*. Test your impressions thoroughly.

God leads your *stops* as well as your *steps!* And your four road-guides serve as a check and balance over against your light "from within" . . . that you may truly "prove (test) the perfect will of God."

Notes

1. Hannah Whitall Smith, *The Christian Secret of a Happy Life* (Old Tappon, New Jersey: Fleming H. Revell Co., 1968), p. 68.

2. J. Sidlow Baxter, *Does God Still Guide?* (Grand Rapids, Michigan: Zondervan Publishing House, 1968), p. 67.

3. J. Wallace Hamilton, *Ride the Wild Horses* (Westwood, New Jersey: Fleming H. Revell Co., 1952), pp. 141-142.

10

Don't Forget Your Fog Lights

Reduced to its barest minimum, the process of divine guidance is to look for your light "from within," then take a second look (when possible) to confirm your inward sense of direction by four outward signs. But there will be those times when you look for guidance . . . and see nothing. It will be just as if the road ahead is enshrouded in fog. Your "head" lights will be inadequate and outward signs indistinguishable. Such times call for special measures. God has provided you with two special sources of light for foggy days. Think of them as fog lights.

Fog Light #1: A Fast

There will be times when your "head" lights will prove inadequate. And when your inward light fails to reveal the will of God, you should resort to a biblical practice called "fasting."

To fast is to voluntarily abstain from food in order to seek God for a special spiritual purpose. Fasting is more than merely going without food. Fasting is a means of divine guidance. That is why Ezra proclaimed a fast—"to seek of him a right way for us" (Ezra 8:21). Fasting and prayer are *coupled* in the Scripture. When the fog is too thick to penetrate by means of normal spiritual enlightenment, God has chosen "fasting and prayer" as a special means of "getting through" to God: "Is not this the fast that I have chosen . . . then shall thy light break forth as the morning . . . then shalt thou call, and the Lord shall answer" (Isa. 58:6-9).

But how does God answer during times of fasting? Isaiah says you will hear God's voice. Does that mean he will speak audibly? Frankly, I once had great difficulty with men who habitually used the phrase, "God told me," or, "God spoke to me." Almost the instant a fellow said "God spoke to me," something inside me automatically seemed to reach up and turn him off. But later I realized such men were merely using Scripture terminology. New Testament Christians told of God speaking to them: "the Lord stood by him, and said" (Acts 23:11).

In fact, the Bible indicates that *all* Christians can hear God's voice. This is a means by which we receive guidance: "My sheep hear my voice . . . and they follow me" (John 10:27). What the New Testament saints most often seemed to indicate was that God spoke to them through the Spirit: "The Spirit said unto Philip" (Acts 8:29). "While Peter thought on the vision, the Spirit said unto him" (Acts 10:19). "As they ministered to the Lord, the Holy Spirit said" (Acts 13:2).

And in the deepest sense of the word I believe the Holy Spirit speaks to us today. But this is not to say he speaks audibly. You do not hear him with the human ear like I would speak to you. Indeed, I have asked three of the finest Christians I know (who often use the term "God told me"), and each of them denied having ever heard God speak to them in an audible voice. How then does the Holy Spirit communicate to us?

The *Holy Spirit* communicates to us through our *human spirit:* "The Spirit itself beareth witness with our spirit" (Rom. 8:16).

The human spirit has a faculty called "intuition" by which you can know things: "And immediately when Jesus *perceived in his spirit* that they so reasoned within themselves" (Mark 2:8, italics added). Jesus perceived this intuitively.

Intuition comes from a Latin root *intueri*, which means to "look in." It denotes a form of perception . . . a nonphysical faculty for observing the essence of something intangible. Your spirit contains an intuitive faculty for knowing.

So the Holy Spirit imparts godly knowledge to a Christian through the intuitive faculty of the human spirit. And (think with me) this knowledge passes . . . from the spirit to the mind . . . by the process of mental verbalization. That is, *the impressions of God are received in the spirit and pass into our human understanding as we verbalize them.* We understand by the use of meaningful words. So, in this sense, we hear God's words. Paul describes this process in his Ephesian letter: "May [God] give unto you the *spirit* of wisdom and revelation in the knowledge of him. The eyes of your *understanding* being enlightened; that ye may know" (Eph. 1:17-18, italics added).

Fasting and prayer increase our sensitivity to God's voice: "As they . . . fasted the Holy Ghost said" (Acts 13:2-3).

Recently it was my privilege to minister in a large church in northern Ohio. During that week the pastor shared a wonderful experience with us. A few years earlier the Federal Government ruled against the type of bonds issued by this church. The judgment required the immediate payoff and retirement of a large bond issue. At the original rate of retirement, the church would have had no problems meeting its payoff schedule. But to immediately pay off an entire bond issue was all but disastrous. The church sold some properties but still lacked over *three million dollars* to meet their immediate need. A lifetime of toil and sacrifice hung in the balance. And the pastor said, "I simply could not determine what God would have me do!"

But he knew how to penetrate the fog. He got alone with God and spent much of a week . . . *in fasting and prayer*. Finally he received a definite impression. Outward signs confirmed it. So he went deeper in debt and borrowed over three hundred thousand dollars. Then he used the borrowed money for such things as television time and thousands of registered letters to explain his need to every person who had ever written them. And his return mail brought back over three million dollars in donations! This is but one experience among the countless times God has granted special enlightenment to those who have sought him through fasting and prayer.

Fog Light #2: A Fleece

As we said, there will be those times when you cannot see the road ahead. However, even if the fog does lift enough for you to see the road in front of you, you still might not be able to see outward signs well enough to *confirm* your direction.

But that is the purpose of your second fog light. When you are unable to confirm your sense of leading with the Scriptures, or the character of God, or circumstances, or your conscience . . . then you may seek God's confirmation through the use of a *fleece*.

This method is called "putting out the fleece" because of an Old

Testament passage where the approach is most clearly described. It will be of great benefit to examine the experience as the Scriptures relate it. Israel was under siege and in desperate straits: "Israel was greatly impoverished because of the Midianites; and the children of Israel cried unto the Lord" (Judg. 6:6). But Gideon, a mighty man of valour, was called of God to deliver the Israelites from their oppression. Immediately upon his call, Gideon entered into service (Judg. 6:25). Later, under the influence of the Holy Spirit, Gideon rallied 32,000 men to do battle against their oppressors. However, Gideon tarried one more time before God . . . to make sure he properly understood: "And Gideon said unto God, If thou wilt save Israel by my hand, *as thou hast said,* Behold, I will put a fleece of wool in the floor; and if the dew be on the fleece only, and it be dry upon the earth beside, then shall I know that thou wilt save Israel by mine hand, *as thou hast said*" (Judg. 6:36-37, italics added).

Gideon wanted to confirm his sense of leading. And God confirmed his words by doing exactly what Gideon asked. Gideon "rose up early on the morrow, and thrust the fleece together, and wringed the dew out of the fleece, a bowl full of water" (Judg. 6:38).

However, this passage has been so misused and abused that we should clearly delineate the pertinent factors which have lasting validity for our guidance today. Let us make some observations:

1. Gideon put out his fleece to "prove" God's will: "Let me prove I pray thee" (Judg. 6:39). As stated in our last chapter, to prove God's guidance *is to test and confirm it.* Gideon had already received a word of direction. Now he was seeking to verify it.

This is much like confirming your inward light by "circumstances," as we discussed in our last chapter. But there is one big difference. When you verify a course of action circumstantially, you ask God to take the initiative and confirm it by any means he chooses. But when you put out a fleece, *you* take the initiative and ask God to do one specific thing as a means of confirming your sense of direction. Naturally, this is a process you will want to reserve for days of spiritual density only.

2. Furthermore, Gideon put out the fleece to seek God's will about an *enormous* decision. The Midianites and the Amalekites had already

driven the children of Israel out of their camps into "the dens which were in the mountains, and caves" (Judg. 6:2). They had encamped against Israel and completely destroyed all its crops. They "destroyed the increase of the earth . . . and left no sustenance for Israel, neither sheep, nor ox" (Judg. 6:4). The Midianites and Amalekites were as "grasshoppers for multitude," without number. And make no mistake about it, "they entered into the land to destroy it" (Judg. 6:5). This was a matter of life and death, and Gideon was to lead Israel out of her precarious condition. It was a decision of consequence.

3. Gideon could hardly believe God actually called *him*. Yet, he did not put out a fleece until he had already attempted to confirm his leading by other means. Indeed, the way he first sought to verify his word from God is a choice example of the formula for a "second look," as suggested in our last chapter:

Gideon sought to confirm what he heard with that previous knowledge which was his *Scripture:* "If the Lord be with us, why then is all this befallen us? and where be all his miracles *which* our fathers told us of, saying, Did not the Lord bring us up from Egypt?" (Judg. 6:13).

Gideon sought to confirm what he heard with the *character of God.* For he asked why a "Mighty God" would use someone as insignificant as himself: "My family is the poorest in the whole tribe of Manasseh, and I am the least thought of in the entire family" (Judg. 6:15, TLB).

Gideon sought to confirm what he heard with the surrounding *circumstances* when he asked for a sign: "If now I have found grace in thy sight, then shew me a sign that thou talkest with me" (Judg. 6:17). (As we have said, this is not a fleece because Gideon did not stipulate what *kind* of a sign. He just asked for any kind of a circumstantial sign. In the case of a fleece, you ask God to do something specific.)

Gideon also sought to confirm what he heard in his *conscience,* for he took no action until he got peace from God about the matter: "And the Lord said unto him, Peace be unto thee. . . . Then Gideon built an altar there unto the Lord, and called it Jehovah-shalom [the peace of God]" (Judg. 6:23-24).

So Gideon attempted to confirm his sense of leading by Scripture, the character of God, circumstances, and conscience . . . but was still uncertain. It was only then he put out a fleece.

4. Gideon was also faced with a limited time factor. For "all the Midianites and Amalekites and the children of the east were gathered together, and went over, and pitched in the valley of Jezreel" (Judg. 6:33). The enemy had formed a vast alliance. They had not crossed into the Jezreel Valley on a holiday outing. This was to be no picnic. They were setting up for battle and soon would attack. Gideon had only a limited time to finalize his decision.

5. It is also important to note that Gideon took action which committed him to his sense of leading before he put out his fleece. He sounded a trumpet and began to gather his army (Judg. 6:34-35). Then, while the thousands were gathering, Gideon asked God to confirm his course of action with a sign. Therefore, to put out a fleece, you must have some inner light on God's will *and begin to obediently follow in that direction.* Then put out your fleece to confirm your leading. As you go, God will confirm your impression from behind you, so to speak: "And thine ears shall hear a word behind thee saying, This is the way, walk ye in it" (Isa. 30:21).

6. Gideon was meticulously objective and honest. He was very careful not to rationalize and read into the sign what he wanted to see in it. This is evident in that, though pressed for time, he waited another day for absolute verification of his fleece. On the first morning the ground was dry and the fleece was wet. But Gideon asked for the opposite to be true on the following morning . . . for the fleece to be dry and the ground to be wet. Some say that Gideon was asking for a "second" sign of verification. However, I view this as *the final verification of the first sign.* Gideon most likely reflected that the rocky threshing floor would, in any case, dry more quickly than the fleece, so the reverse would truly be more remarkable and indeed finalize the sign as a divine verification.

You must be equally as objective and honest in seeking a sign from God. It is so easy to see what you most *want* to see. It's possible to read in more than is really there and jump at a hoped-for conclusion. Gideon committed himself to a course of action, then waited two days for *absolute* verification of his fleece. Real faith will trust God for a complete, genuine verification of a fleece!

Having made these observations, let me say God still honors a fleece

. . . under proper conditions. Several months ago I began to seek God for a sound system for our daughters' use when they sing in our conferences from night to night. A voice teacher told us this would be a "must" to preserve their voices. But God impressed me not to go in debt to buy it but to pray through until one was provided. Three months rolled by without a dollar for it. And just last week I began to face the fact that I had no real corroborative evidence from God to confirm my prayerful quest. So I finally felt led to put out a fleece. I asked God: "Dear Lord, I have acted on the assumption that you want me to seek this sound system by prayer and faith rather than to borrow the money for it. If this is your will, would you *confirm* it by having some money arrive for it by next week? And if not, I will seek to secure a system by some other means." Within a week we had received $275 in donations from various sources!

A friend of mine travels a great deal. He felt God leading him to sell a small rent house and purchase a motor home for his family to travel with him. He checked out various types of motor homes and found one type which suited their needs. But his rent house did not sell. He thoroughly sought God for confirmation about the matter and finally put out the following fleece: "Lord, if you wish me to continue trying to sell our rent house in order to purchase a motor home, I want to put out a fleece and ask that someone contact me within a week and express interest in purchasing my rent house. Even if someone contacts me who is interested, I will consider this a confirmation of my sense of direction."

The next week a man not only approached him but traded a motor home for the rent house . . . just the type of motor home God had led him to secure.

Under the proper conditions, God will still honor a fleece. Gideon set a precedence. So don't put out a fleece until you can say yes to the following questions:

(1) Do you already have a sense of direction, and is this fleece to confirm it?

(2) Is this a significant decision, of real consequence?

(3) Have you already sought to confirm your course of action with your map . . . *the Scriptures*, your red lights . . . *God's character*, your road signs . . . *circumstances*, and your compass . . . *conscience?*

(4) Do you face a limited time factor? Must you know now?

(5) Have you begun to follow in the direction of your leading and committed yourself to that course of action?

(6) Will you be meticulously honest and objective, refusing to accept anything as confirmation of your "fleece" unless it *clearly fulfills* your specific request for a sign?

Perhaps this chapter will find you in a quandary about God's will for your life. You have really taken the time to seek his guidance, but you have drawn a blank.

Don't forget your fog lights! God has provided two special means of enlightenment for just such times of severe spiritual density. (1) When your "head" lights are inadequate to reveal the way and you have no inner sense of direction, you fast! (2) When you gain an inner sense of direction but your outward signs are indistinguishable and you can't *confirm* your leading, you put out a fleece!

The order is very significant. Be careful not to put out a *fleece* when you should *fast*. That's how Israel abused the "fleece" method. In Exodus 17 Israel put out a fleece and asked for a hurried sign in order to see if God would provide light at all. And the Bible referred to this as a presumptuous act. They "tempted" God (Ex. 17:7). The Israelites put out a *fleece* when they should have *fasted*, and God was displeased. Don't put out a fleece indiscriminately, seeking signs as a constant and instant source of guidance and in place of your lights "from within." This is what God had in mind when he said, "A wicked and adulterous generation seeketh after a sign" (Matt. 16:4). There are two separate conditions which require two different actions. When inner light is inadequate, you fast; when outward signs are indistinguishable, you put out a fleece!

Your two fog lights are a means of humbling yourself. Remember this about fog lights: They are always mounted low on an automobile, for the fog is thinner close to the ground. Likewise, your spiritual fog lights are to bring you low, to humble you. David said, "I humbled my soul with fasting" (Ps. 35:13).

No one struts like a peacock into God's will. But heaven honors those bent low in a humble, earnest quest for guidance: "The meek will he guide in judgment: and the meek will he teach his way" (Ps. 25:9).

11

The Sign of a God-guided Life

What is the sign of a God-guided life? Out of all the many dividends of living in accordance with God's will, what is the one most obvious effect? What, more than anything else, is evidence that you have learned to find and follow God's will?

The hallmark of a God-guided life *is the ability to give God thanks for everything that happens to you.* Paul lists several results of a God-guided life in his Colossian letter. He seems to set forth the steps to a fully guided life when he shares his prayer that they might learn to *walk*, "that ye might walk worthy of the Lord"; to *work*, "being fruitful in every good work"; to be spiritually *wise*, "increasing in the knowledge of God"; to *wait*, "strengthened unto all patience"; and to *worship*, "giving thanks" (Col. 1:9-12). The last and crowning result is the ability to give thanks!

Paul is even more specific in his first Thessalonian letter: *"No matter what happens, always be thankful, for this is God's will for you* who belong to Christ Jesus" (1 Thess. 5:18, TLB, italics added). A Christian in God's will can be thankful for everything, "no matter what happens."

Be deeply honest at this point. How sure are you of God's guidance in your life? How certain are you that God's will is the perfect plan for your life? Are you positive enough to thank God for every single experience . . . no matter what happens?

The full effect of a God-guided life, and your ability to give thanks in everything, hinges upon your faith. You must trust God to pull it off in your daily experience. That is, you must believe God is capable of accomplishing his will in your life. David emphasized this aspect of guidance. He said you must not only commit yourself to God's way, but you must trust God to bring his will and plan to pass: "Commit thy way unto the Lord; *trust also in him;* and he shall bring it to pass" (Ps. 37:5, italics added).

The fact is you *can* trust God to guide you. And such faith rests on the solid foundation of two biblical principles:

The Principle of Correction

Your trust in God's guidance should be based upon his ability to *correct* you when you willfully go astray. One of the most treacherous perils of your Christian journey will be the enticing bypaths along your route. The grass always looks greener along the road that turns away. And you will never entirely subdue your wayward heart this side of heaven. It's like the line of an old hymn: "Prone to wander, Lord, I feel it!"

Christians stray. We forever turn aside from God's will. Sometimes we stray far. Dazzled by the heady exhilaration of worldly patronage, blinded by the glittering lights of sin's way, or transfixed by the lure of earthly pleasures, we would journey endlessly on in our waywardness *so long as we felt all was well:* "I spake unto thee in thy prosperity; but thou saidst, I will not hear" (Jer. 22:21).

But all is never well, when your all *excludes* God's will for your life . . . and *includes* nothing more than temporary pleasures along a bypath to nowhere. So God intercedes. He chastises. He disciplines you in your wrong. But he does this not to punish you *for* your sins (a wrong concept of chastisement), rather to turn you *from* them: "Blessed is the man whom thou chastenest, O Lord . . . judgment shall return unto righteousness: and all the upright in heart will follow it" (Ps. 94:12-15).

Chastisement is remedial, not retributive; it is to restore, not to retaliate. It is God's way of "planting the flag of truth within the fortress of a rebel soul." Chastisement is God's *roadblock:* "I'll block the road before. . . . Then she will think, "I might as well return . . ." (Hos. 2:6-7, TLB). This represents God's determined and faithful effort to circumvent, to cut short a willful plunge downward . . . away from his will. Nevertheless there are some Christians, unheeding and unhampered, whose rebellion must run its course. The prodigal son never "came to himself" until his riotous road dead-ended in a hog pen!

But the severity of chastisement is measured by the persistency of your rebellion. It ranges from a *sting of conscience* "being convicted by their own conscience" (John 8:9): to the *sending of sickness,* "for this cause many are weak and sickly among you" (1 Cor. 11:30).

C. S. Lewis described his experience something like this:

> I am progressing along the path of life until I get side-tracked by some *absorption,* a bit of work that tickles my vanity today, a holiday or a new book. Suddenly a stab of abdominal pain threatens to send the whole pack of cards tumbling down. At first I am overwhelmed for all my little happinesses look like broken toys. Then, slowly, and reluctantly, bit by bit, I try to bring myself into the frame of mind that I should be at all times. I remind myself that all these toys were never intended to possess my heart, that my only real treasure is Christ. For a while, then, I become constantly dependent upon God and draw my strength from the right sources. But the moment the threat is withdrawn, my whole nature might leap back to the toys. Thus the need for chastisement is only too clear. God has led me for but forty-eight hours and then only by dint of taking everything else away from me. Let him but sheathe that sword for a moment and I behave like a puppy when the hated bath is over—I shake myself as dry as I can and race off to require my comfortable dirtiness, if not in the nearest manure heap, at least in the nearest flower bed.[1]

Yes, as severe as chastisement can be, at times, there is no end to our need of it:

> Now obviously no "chastening" seems pleasant at the time. . . . Yet when it is all over we can see that it has quietly produced the fruit of real goodness. . . . So tighten your loosening grip and steady your wavering hand . . . *Don't wander away from the path but forge steadily onward* (Heb. 12:11-13, Phillips).

But not every hardship is chastisement. Not by any means. Much, if not most of the time, you do God's will in a matter, and your action will lead to problems. Such difficulties are often a test of your faith. "These trials are only to test your faith, to see whether or not it is strong and pure" (1 Pet. 1:7, TLB).

The question is often asked: "How can I determine when a difficulty is chastisement or when it is allowed by God as a test of my faith?" By the very nature of chastisement, you can recognize it. God does not correct his children to punish *for* sin, but to awaken you to a wrong course of action and turn you *from* it. God chastises to "show you where you are wrong" (Heb. 12:5, TLB). It would destroy the very purpose and meaning of God's correction, if you were incapable of recognizing it. In his own way, *God will make the sensitive and earnest Christian aware when trouble comes in the form of chastisement.* Like a wise father, God will always let you know the reason for a spanking. If you see no obvious connection between your trouble and a sin . . . press on and consider your difficulty a test of faith. When the tribulation that befalls you makes you aware of a wrong course of action, you should turn from your wrongdoing to do God's will. It is as simple as that.

But there is another principle upon which you should rest your faith that God is able to guide you.

The Principle of Compensation

Your trust in God's guidance should be based upon God's sovereign ability to accomplish his will *through* your mistaken assessment of it.

Suppose you do make a wrong decision. So what! God is not limited by your inability to discern his will. No human act is final. Even when you make a mistake and misjudge his will, God can meet you at that point and work something good out of your error. God has promised to do exactly that: "Moreover we know that to those who love God, who are called according to his plan, everything that happens fits into a pattern for good" (Rom. 8:28, Phillips).

I recall Leslie Weatherhead telling about visiting an Oriental bazaar where he came upon a weaver of fine rugs. Actually there were about a dozen separate rugs stretched on frames. An apprentice was seated at each frame busily weaving brightly colored rugs of beautiful design. The old master weaver was standing back behind the line of apprentices, superintending their work. As Dr. Weatherhead's party looked on, a young apprentice stopped his weaving. He lifted a hand, rather apprehensively, and motioned toward the master weaver. He had made an error. The old weaver walked over and stood behind the young apprentice for an instant, quickly surmising his mistake. Motioning for the boy to get up, the master took his seat. He studied the design intently.

But rather than unravel the mistake, he began weaving. *And the master used the mistake as part of a brand-new design which he wove into the rug.* The final design was more exquisite than the original!

God's sovereignty is not demonstrated in that he acts to prevent Christians from ever making a mistake. (Thank God, for this would rob us of free will and render us mere puppets.) God's sovereignty is evidenced in that he can take your mistake and compensate for it by weaving it into something for his glory and your good. I call this God's "compensational providence." God is actively superintending every advantageous and adverse experience in your Christian life, working them together to a good end!

The Scriptures refer to a time when Paul missed God's will for his life. He was so intent upon fulfilling what he *thought* God wanted him to do that he misinterpreted God's guidance.

You see, Paul had a mistaken conviction that it was God's will for him to go to Jerusalem, "And now I am going to Jerusalem, drawn there irresistibly by the Holy Spirit, not knowing what awaits me" (Acts 20:22, TLB). Paul thought the Holy Spirit was leading him in this direction.

However, a few days later, the ship in which he journeyed docked at Tyre. Paul went ashore, found the local believers, and stayed with them for a week. Some of these disciples spoke to Paul, as the Bible says, "through the Spirit, that he should not go up to Jerusalem" (Acts 21:4).

Paul was wrong about what he thought was the Holy Spirit's leading. And the Spirit used other Christians to inform him of his error. But Paul was intent on having it his way, "we departed and went our way" (Acts 21:5).

However, at Paul's next stop, in Caesarea, he lodged in the home of Philip. While there, the Holy Spirit dramatically spoke through a prophet named Agabus, and Paul received his second warning not to go up to Jerusalem—"He took Paul's belt, bound his own feet and hands with it and said, The Holy Spirit declares, 'So shall the owner of this belt be bound by the Jews in Jerusalem and turned over to the Romans'" (Acts 21:11, TLB).

Furthermore, each and every Christian leader at Caesarea, which included Philip and Luke, "besought him not to go up to Jerusalem" (Acts 21:12). But when Paul would not be dissuaded, the disciples gave up and prayed that God's will would be accomplished . . . even though Paul was wrong (Acts 21:14).

Paul blew it. In the face of three attempts by the Holy Spirit to change his mind, Paul stepped out of God's will for his life while doing what he "thought" was right.

Paul was not without a sincere purpose. He was not void of a pure motive. His dogged determination was based upon several good reasons for going to Jerusalem: (1) He was going there to carry a gift that had been gathered among the Gentile churches, for the poor saints in Jerusalem. (2) He was motivated by the master-passion of his life, the desire to bring together the Jews and Gentiles into a consciousness of their oneness in Jesus Christ. (3) The time of Paul's arrival in Jerusalem was to be the Feast of Pentecost when several million Jews would be crowded into the city . . . to whom he could witness.

But this illustration from Paul's life merely underlines a danger in terms of finding and following God's will for your life. In one sense, it is the most genuine and dedicated Christian that is likely to miss God's will. Such a Christian is so deeply moved by the cause of Christ that he commits himself with abandon. He grabs a task and holds on with all the tenacity of a bulldog. But need never constitutes a call. You must always take a "second look" and confirm God's leading. By blind devotion to a *good* course, you can miss God's *best* use of your life in a given situation . . . as, in this case, Paul did.

Furthermore, when Paul journeyed to Jerusalem outside of God's will, *he lost his perspective and made a second mistake.* His arrival caused quite a stir among the Jews who resented his preoccupation with Gentile Christians. So the Jewish leaders successfully persuaded Paul to compromise his conviction about a matter. The Jerusalem elders asked Paul to join several other Jewish men and go through the ritual necessary to fulfill a Nazarite vow. They reasoned that such a course of action would vindicate Jewish rites and ceremonies and contradict reports that Paul had personally abandoned the observance of them. This was dishonest. At Antioch Paul had rebuked Peter for doing this. Now he was being asked to do the same.

In tender and sympathetic terms, let us be reminded that Paul had *nothing* personally to gain by consenting to this request. He did so. But his action was that of a man who earnestly desired to do anything to win his brethren. He was motivated by the same desire which caused him to write: "Oh, Israel, my people! Oh, my Jewish brothers! How I long for you to come to Christ. My heart is heavy within me and I grieve bitterly day and night because of you . . . it is no mere pretense when I say that I would be willing to be forever damned if that would save you" (Rom. 9:1-3, TLB).

But Paul *was* wrong. He was so wrong that G. Campbell Morgan was moved to exclaim: "I hold that Paul made the greatest mistake of his ministry on this occasion." [2] Paul's action cost him the very opportunity of witness to his brethren that he was seeking. The Jews resented his presence in the Temple, so they threw him out and beat him, and he was jailed.

It was at this point that God moved in and began to work out a new design. Later, as Paul sat in jail and pored over his error, the Master came and stood by his side: "The Lord stood by him, and said, Be of good cheer, Paul: for as thou hast testified of me in Jerusalem, so must thou bear witness of me in Rome" (Acts 23:11). The Master was going to weave Paul's mistake into a new design. He was going to use Paul's imprisonment as a means of getting him transferred to Rome . . . *from where Paul would bear a witness throughout the world.*

Perhaps you are trusting God to lead you about a matter right now. Let me ask, are you anxious or apprehensive about finding God's will in this matter? Do you doubt you can find his will? If you had your answer and knew God's will, would you rejoice over the answer any more than you are doing right now, by faith? If so . . . your faith is lacking. You need to *trust* God!

Always find God's way . . . then follow it, in full confidence that you have done the will of God. Of course there will be those times when you miss God's will. You can step out of God's will out of careless ignorance. You may be rash and impatient, presumptuously rationalizing God's will about a matter. At other times you will simply rebel and be stubborn enough to do what you want without consulting God. But God will chastise you. Faithfully and unsparingly, God will act to plant a flag of truth inside your rebellious soul to warn you of your foolish course, and return you to his will and blessings. This is the *principle of correction*.

There will also be those occasions when you miss God's will even in the process of earnestly seeking to do right. But God will exercise his transcendent sovereignty by working your mistake into something which can be beneficial to your course and his cause. This is the *principle of compensation*.

When you begin to live in the reality of these two principles, a great deal of the anxiety, fear, and doubts of life will vanish. Confident that your life is in God's will, there is nothing to worry about. You will be able to rest in God's divine superintending providence. For he is actively working out his plan in your life . . . to his glory and your good. Thus, the sign of your ability to find and follow God's will is *your willingness to be thankful for everything in life* . . . no matter what happens!

Notes

1. C. S. Lewis, *The Problem of Pain* (New York: Macmillan Co., 1962), pp. 106-107.
2. G. Campbell Morgan, *The Acts of the Apostles* (Westwood, N.J.: Fleming H. Revell Co., 1924), p. 485.

12
Rules for the Road

A principle which runs like a thread throughout the woof and warp of all these chapters is that *God's will can be perfectly discerned only as you maintain an active life of sacrificial, spiritual service.* According to Romans 12:1-2, they who present their bodies a "living sacrifice" can "prove . . . the perfect will of God." Don't misunderstand. You can know God's will about a lot of things apart from a commitment to do his will. But you will never be able to prove God's "perfect" will and fulfill God's best plan for your life apart from denying yourself, taking up your cross daily, and following him . . . as a living sacrifice, in spiritual service.

This being the case, that God's will can be perfectly discerned only as you maintain a life of sacrificial, spiritual service, then how do you maintain such a life? How do you stay on the road?

There are several trouble spots to watch for in terms of Christian service. And the following rules will prepare you to cope with them. Call them *rules for the road.*

Rule #1: Check the Attitude Quotient

On the slope of Long's Peak in Colorado lies the ruin of a veritable forest giant. Naturalists say the tree stood for four hundred years; it was a seedling when Columbus landed in America; it had been struck by lightning fourteen times; the avalanches and storms of four centuries thundered past it. But what impressed me most was that, in the end, beetles killed the tree. The little things spoiled it. How like some stalwarts of our faith who withstand the onslaught of a hundred different kinds of difficulties in order to remain faithful in their service to God, but in the end they blow their testimony because *an attitude was showing.*

Here we come, presumptuous and obtrusive, rushing, pushing, and fuming along the way. Full of vainglory and condescending pride, we fling our service to people like coins are flung to beggars. Or we ooze with a kind of soft, oily, sentimental gushiness that is supposed to resemble love. And with such attitudes showing, our effectiveness dies.

As we have said, Romans 12:6-8 lists the various areas in which God gives special enablements for service. But this passage also establishes certain prerequisites for exercising these spiritual gifts. The Scriptures list *one requirement* for *each enablement.* There is a stipulation placed upon each gift:

> Let us prophesy *according to the proportion of faith;* or ministry, *let us wait on our ministering;* or he that teacheth, *on teaching;* or he that exhorteth, *on exhortation:* he that giveth, *let him do it with simplicity;* he that ruleth, *with diligence,* he that sheweth mercy, *with cheerfulness* (Rom. 12:6-8, requirements italicized).

These requirements serve to emphasize the *attitude* in which you serve. The exercise of a spiritual gift is commendable, a mark of spiritual concern on your part. But the fact that you care enough to serve God as he enables is still more a privilege than a sacrifice, and the proper exercise of your spiritual gift carries with it the requirement that you serve in the right attitude. The execution of your gift does not exempt you from the necessity of serving God in the proper spirit. A foul disposition can sabotage the effect of any deed.

How well I recall a leading church member whose general attitude was so negative that another member said to me: "I believe he is the only person I ever met who could make me mad while giving me $10,000."

Take an attitude check! Consider the examples of Paul in Romans 12:6-8. If you *prophesy,* do it "to the proportion of faith." That is, limit your inspired utterances to those things you deeply believe God would have you say . . . be earnest and honest! If you *minister, teach, or exhort,* "wait on" these activities. That is, give of yourself to them; put all you've got into them . . . do not engage in them casually or indifferently. If you *give,* do it with "simplicity." That is, give of yourself without fanfare, with no strings attached, unpretentiously, as if it were nothing; almost anonymously . . . not like the hypocrites who had them blow trumpets to announce their gifts (Matt. 6:2). If you *rule*, lead with "diligence." That is, lead with zeal and consistency . . . as opposed to inertness, carelessness, or procrastination. If you *show mercy*, do so in an attitude of "cheerfulness." That is, extend a helping hand enthusiastically, and lovingly . . . not begrudgingly, as if you were "put upon."

In every possible service situation where you exercise a spiritual gift, there is a proper corresponding attitude, apart from which the effect of your deed is lessened . . . if not lost. In a recent conversation, I recall a lady who lifted her head in a gesture of self-importance and with exaggerated pretense remarked, "God has given me a gift for singing!" Somehow her announcement failed to excite me about the prospect of hearing her. Remember, the Bible says: "Dead flies will cause even a bottle of perfume to stink" (Eccl. 10:1, TLB). So if a proven gift becomes ineffective, the first thing to do is examine your enablement and ask: "Have I exercised my gift in the proper attitude?"

Rule #2: Check the Balance Factor

One of the most important factors in terms of God's will for your service has to do with *balance*. There is a basic flaw within human nature: *Man is forever doing one thing to the neglect of something else.* We *go*, to the neglect of *withdrawing;* or we are *concerned*, to the neglect of *trusting;* or we *take*, to the neglect of *giving;* or we *prepare*, to the neglect of *praying;* or we emphasize *programs*, to the neglect of *persons.* It seems we never quite get our balance!

Surely, even the most casual observer of Christian history will recognize what I choose to call the "pendulum principle." Much like a pendulum, our emphasis forever swings too far in one direction. Then we swing back to emphasize that which we have neglected . . . but to the extreme, so that we slight that which we have previously overemphasized. And we keep swinging back and forth from one extreme to the other. It seems we have a natural tendency toward preoccupation, an affinity for tangents. We are so like Peter who *presumptuously* drew his sword in combat for the Lord at one moment, then *passively denied* his Lord the next.

Most likely, the reasons for this inclination are varied and complex. Certainly we are so spiritually impoverished that when we do stumble into a real spiritual experience we go after it with all the relish and abandonment of a starving man after bread . . . and perhaps our momentum carries us too far.

But I would venture a "holy hunch" that the causative factor behind the "pendulum principle" is a lack of *disciplined spiritual action*. You see, balance comes by disciplined action . . . of the most consistent kind. If you are not *acting*, you will soon find yourself *reacting*, and when you are merely reacting to life, you usually respond late. Consequently, you overcompensate to the opposite extreme and go too far. One is said to "strike a balance." This speaks of action. Disciplined, consistent action eliminates reaction so that life won't oscillate in a pendulum-type path.

Imbalance often results from a failure to take proper action with regard to the following factors:

1. *The Both/And Balance*

The exercise of a spiritual gift should always receive priority in terms of your activities of service but never to the point of preoccupation and neglect of other duties. When you weigh the significance of exercising your gift, as over against the performance of other duties, it should never be an *either/or*, but a *both/and* proposition.

Jesus established the "Both/And Balance" when he said: "These ought ye to have done, and not to leave the other undone" (Luke 11:42). I believe Jesus would say the same about *three* oft-recurring tendencies of those who exercise spiritual gifts. You will want to take action against:

(1) the tendency to execute your gift to the total neglect of the other six areas of spiritual enablement. Mark this down: All of us are responsible for serving God along the line of all seven areas of supernatural enablement:

All are to prophesy: "Every man praying or *prophesying* (1 Cor. 11:4, all italics in these verses added).

All are to minister: "Perfecting the saints, for the work of the *ministry*" (Eph. 4:12).

All are to teach: "Ye ought to be *teachers*" (Heb. 5:12).

All are to exhort: "*Exhort* one another daily" (Heb. 3:13).

All are to give: "First *gave* their own selves" (2 Cor. 8:5).

All are to rule: "*Ruling* their children and their own houses" (1 Tim. 3:12).

All are to be merciful: "Blessed are the *merciful*" (Matt. 5:7). While majoring in one of these areas, you should practice them all!

Also, concerning the "Both/And Balance," you will want to take action against:

(2) the tendency to become so enamored with the exercise of a spiritual gift that you would neglect your God-given *natural* talents. Again, it is true that your gift deserves priority, but God will also hold you accountable for the use of every natural talent (Matt. 25:15-28).

As we mentioned before, it is reasonable to assume that God will give you gifts *commensurate with* and *complementary to* your natural talent. Let me give an example. An intrinsic, vital part of the Richard Hogue Crusade team has been the youth-oriented singing group, "Dove." Though constantly misunderstood and grossly unappreciated by some adults, these young people have already poured five years of their lives into crusade ministry. They have each remained single, maintained lives of spotless spiritual purity, and devoted themselves entirely to God's service. I have never known anyone more committed. And God has used them mightily. I believe one of the group has the gift of prophecy, one the gift of exhortation, and one a double gift of prophecy and ruling, and one the gift of mercy—but all of them execute their gifts as helpers . . . along with and through the medium of music. Do you see, they exercise their *gift* by the use of *natural talents*. Your talents will often be the vessel through which your spiritual gifts will be exercised. It isn't a matter of gifts *or* talents, but gifts *and* talents.

You will also want to take action against:

(3) getting so puffed up with a false sense of self-importance as to think your gift is more important than your brother's. Paul specifically corrected this false impression in his letter to the Corinthian church. In the very passage which leads to the listing of the various means of *executing* gifts (1 Cor. 12:12-28), Paul stated:

> Suppose the whole body were an eye—then how would you hear? Or if your whole body were just one big ear, how could you smell

anything? . . . The eye can never say to the hand, "I don't need you." The head can't say to the feet, "I don't need you." And some of the parts that seem weakest and least important are really the most necessary (1 Cor. 12:17,21-22, TLB).

Perhaps our balance can come from the realization that your gift is only grand for you because you *are* you! Your neighbor does not necessarily need such a gift. Nor could he use it. Why look in disdain at the other man's gift? His is right for him. Yours is right for you. Neither of you could function best with the other's gift. Ron Dunn said it something like this: The Head of the body looked condescendingly down to the Big Toe one night and said, "Toe, you really haven't got it *all* yet! You need to seek the gift of seeing." Now, suppose the Big Toe prays, and prays, and prays until God finally agrees to give him the gift of seeing. What would he see? . . . Just the inside of a dirty sock!

These are the most oft-recurring ways of losing your "Both/And Balance." In short, do not exercise your spiritual gift: to the disregard of the other six areas; to the discard of natural talents; to the disdain of the gift of others.

But *imbalance* can *also* result from a failure to take action with regard to your:

2. *Inward/Outward Balance*

You must always be careful that your *inward purity* is equal to your *outward service*.

Jesus established the Inward/Outward Balance in lieu of the Pharisees' tendency to be hypocritical. The Pharisees did good deeds apart from proper consideration of inward holiness: "Even so ye also *outwardly* appear righteous unto men, but *within* ye are full of hypocrisy and iniquity" (Matt. 23:28, italics added).

Be careful not to get so involved in service that you neglect such things as prayer, confession, study of God's Word . . . those things which lead to a Christlike life. So often the world around us fails to recognize the *good* we do because of the *bad* we are!

Rule #3: Check the Power Source

The third major trouble spot in Christian service is a never-ending tendency to serve in the strength of our own ability rather than in God's. Peter urged us to be careful about the power source for our service: "As every man hath received the gift, even so minister the same one to another, as good stewards . . . *let him do it as of the ability which God giveth*" (1 Pet. 4:10-11, italics added). You must always serve in the strength of God!

God has always expected service from his children. One of the reasons God delivered the Israelites from their slavery in Egypt was that they might more freely serve him. God stated this several times:

"Let my people go, that they may serve me" (Ex. 7:16).

"Let my people go, that they may serve me" (Ex. 8:20).

"Let my people go, that they may serve me" (Ex. 9:1).

"Let my people go, that they may serve me" (Ex. 9:13).

But, even after their deliverance, the Israelites failed miserably in their service to God. And if I had to state in one sentence their greatest problem in serving God, I would say the Israelites *were just too handy*. The Bible says they "rejoiced in the works of their own *hands*" (Acts 7:41, italics added). In the incident to which this verse refers, Israel rejected their leader and set about to make an image of worship by their own doing (Ex. 32:1-9). They thought of religious service in terms of their own *ability*. They did not really need God (so they thought), and they set about to establish their own righteousness and erected an altar . . . to and for themselves. But God was not in it. In fact, God destroyed it (Ex. 32:20).

Interestingly enough, Moses failed once to deliver Israel because of the same problem—*he was just too handy:* "He supposed . . . that God *by his hand* would deliver them" (Acts 7:25, italics added). Though an Israelite, Moses had been reared within the palace of Egypt. He was quite outstanding. The Bible said he was "learned in all the wisdom of the Egyptians, and was mighty in words and in deeds" (Acts 7:22). One day he set out to deliver his brother Israelites from their bondage. He came upon an Egyptian who was mistreating an Israelite. To avenge the Israelite, Moses killed and buried the Egyptian. But strong winds blew the sand away from the grave, the body was uncovered, his deed was discovered, and he fled for his life. Moses tried to lead Israel by his own ability, but the Israelites *rejected* him (Ex. 2:15). Moses fled!

However, forty years later God *did* call Moses to lead Israel out of Egypt: "This Moses whom they refused, saying, Who made thee a ruler . . . the same did God send to be a ruler and a deliverer" (Acts 7:35).

Moses was a changed man. He was not so handy now. God found him on the "backside of the desert." And when God called him to lead Israel he was very reluctant to accept, saying: "Who am I, that I should go?" (Ex. 3:11). Quite a difference in this Moses, from the presumptuous young man who swaggered out of a palace to help God out forty years before.

Perhaps the reticence of Moses was most vividly focused when he reminded God of Israel's former unwillingness to follow him and asked what *authority* he would have. God's answer was superb. God asked Moses, *"What is that in thine hand?"* (Ex. 4:2). Moses replied, "a rod." It was a common shepherd's rod. Moses had been reduced to a humble sheepherder tending his father-in-law's flock on the backside of the desert. So now all Moses had in his hand was a common shepherd's rod, and notice, God told Moses to throw even it down: "Cast it on the ground" (Ex. 4:3). Gone is the finery of palace dress. Gone is the power of palace privilege. Gone is the princely prestige. Gone are the friends in high circles. Gone is the strong young body. Gone is the razor-sharp mind, fresh from Egyptian schooling. Gone is the zeal to avenge. Gone is the self-confidence. *And now, even his shepherd's* rod must go! Never forget this moment. Visualize Moses as he stands empty-handed before God, and fix that picture in your mind. Moses, as he is seen in just that instant, is the lasting image of the kind of man God uses. You must throw down every single thing in your hand. God calls the empty-handed. Surrender your self-sufficiency. When Moses threw down the rod, it became a *snake*, a symbol of the satanic nature of mere human ability in God's service. You see, Satan will seldom hinder you from doing things *for* God, for that prevents God from doing things *through* you . . . and God's doings are of such greater magnitude!

Next, God told Moses to pick up the snake. Moses did, and it became a rod in his hand. But it was no longer a shepherd's rod; now it had become *"the rod of God"* (Ex. 4:20). Before it had been a man's rod:

"It could do no more than a man could do and could strike no harder than the strength of the man whose hand held it." [1] Now the snake of self-sufficiency is out of it. It has become the rod of God. Moses now raises the rod in battle and the Amalekites are routed. Moses lifts it to strike a rock, and water miraculously gushes forth. Yes, and Moses holds the rod over the Red Sea and the waters roll back, allowing the Israelites to cross over on dry ground. Then the waters reconverged on Egypt's pursuing troops, to drown them. Israel is delivered from Egypt! Ian Thomas pointed out that when Moses tried to tackle the job he could not successfully bury even one Egyptian. But, "when *God* tackled the job, he buried the whole lot of them in the Red Sea." [2]

It is not ability but availability that qualifies a man for God's service. God will refuse everything in your hand. There is nothing in your hand of natural strength that can accomplish God's work. But if you cast it all down at his feet, God will take the snake of self-effort out of it. Then a mere shepherd's rod can become the rod of God.

God would never commission you to carry out his high-powered tasks with firecracker ability. That's crazy! Sam Shoemaker said, "the church without power is a factory for hypocrites." [3] In other words, for God to demand more than you can produce makes it inevitable that you "fake it" as a Christian, since you would be incapable of fulfilling his wishes.

God *will* provide power for all that he calls us to do, but a word is in order as to *what kind of power*. Long ago I recall reading a definition by Canon Streeter who said: *Power is the ability to accomplish purpose.* This definition is actually quite profound. It touches on the essence of real power. For example, an ax is a powerful tool for smashing things; but for the purpose of shaving, it has definite limitations. Correspondingly, *the kinds of power God provides will differ from person to person, and from task to task . . . depending upon God's purpose in each case.*

For the gift of prophecy, God's power might be demonstrated in the ability to find the mind of God concerning the spiritual matters of life and communicate that message to others in a most forceful manner. But for the gift of ministry, the provision of power might come in terms of a keen perception about practical tasks and an ability to work in harmony with others, even if your co-laborer is obnoxious.

On the one hand, for someone whose basic *enabling* is a gift of showing mercy and who is led to *execute* that gift in a ministry of "healing," God's power might be provided in terms of an unusual ability to prevail in intercessory prayer. On the other hand, for a person whose same basic *enabling* is a gift for showing mercy but who *executes* that gift as a "helper," the provision of God's power might come in terms of the infinite patience it takes to "nurse" a smelly, thick-tongued winebibber back to sobriety. Power is the ability to accomplish purpose, and God's purpose pertains to the *minute* as well as to the *magnificent*, *ministry* as well as *message*, and the *monotonous* as well as the *miraculous*.

God *will* provide power for all he calls us to do, but another word is in order concerning the *source* of that power. The agent of God's power is the Holy Spirit. The Holy Spirit is the power source for all God intends to accomplish in this world. It is a basic law of spiritual service that every demand upon your life is a demand upon the Spirit within you.

It should go without saying, then, that you need to be "filled with the Spirit" for the full effect of a spiritual gift. Indeed, the filling of the Spirit is most basically that—*an empowering for service.* If you are among the spiritually "unemployed," you won't need to be filled (empowered) with the Spirit. You won't use it! God won't waste it! You won't get it! Many are the people who have prayed to be filled and experienced nothing . . . because they did not seek power for service.

This book is written upon the assumption that anyone so interested in serving God as to want a spiritual gift will be willing to learn and experience the "filling of the Spirit." This author has written a book which covers that subject entitled *Journey into Fullness.* You will want to consult such a book if you need special help at this point.

However, it so happens that we have already discussed the most vital single step to a "filling of the Spirit" in chapter 3 of this book. It has been my observation that most Christians will experience a Spirit-filled life in the course of following the instructions at the close of that chapter with regard to *consecration.* Consecration is the fun-

damental essential for the Spirit's empowering. For when you consider
the entire scope of biblical teaching on this subject, the one consistent
fact is that a consecrated life has always been the prime prerequisite
in preparation for the Holy Spirit's power. A choice example of this
is the preparation required for the priest of the Old Testament to qualify
him for Temple service. He had to be *consecrated*.

But a priest could not consecrate his own life. The blood of a sacrificial
animal was shed. Then *the priest would identify himself with the sacrifice*
in that the animal's blood was applied to his body and garments. Then
anointing oil was sprinkled upon him. "And thou shalt take of *the blood*
that is upon the altar, and of the *anointing oil*, and sprinkle it upon
Aaron" (Ex. 29:21, italics added). Both the *blood* and the *oil* were
significant: The sacrificial blood brought full cleansing from sin; and
the anointing oil represented the Holy Spirit's power which is provided
in response to that cleansing.

Therefore, to "consecrate" your life is to *submit it, without sin, for
God's use. And such a life will know the empowering of God's Spirit.*

Your Part in Consecration

God's Part in Consecration

Ruthlessly reject sins in your life
by *"reckoning"* yourself dead to
them (Rom. 6:11) . . . just as instructed in chapter 3.

And the Holy Spirit will carry out
the execution (Rom. 8:13). But
*refusal to cooperate with the
Spirit in this way means you will
habitually commit sins of commission (things done which you
should not do) which will "grieve
the Holy Spirit"* (Eph. 4:30).

Relentlessly pursue righteousness by *"yielding"* to specific
tasks God impresses you to do
(Rom. 6:13) . . . just as instructed
in chapter 3.

And the Holy Spirit will quicken
(enable) you (Rom. 8:11). But
*refusal to cooperate with the
Spirit in this way means you will
habitually commit sins of omis-
sion (things you should do but
don't) which will "quench" the
Holy Spirit* (1 Thess. 5:19). These
refusals to cooperate with the
Spirit are the very two things the
Bible admonishes you *not* to do

in relation to the Spirit: "Grieve not the Spirit" (Eph. 4:30). "Quench not the Spirit" (1 Thess. 5:19).

Therefore, a consecrated life complies with these two negative admonitions with regard to the Spirit. The Spirit will fill the life of a Christian who will not "grieve" or "quench" him. And this is why I say most "consecrated" Christians will be Spirit-filled.

God will empower a consecrated life. The evidence of that power will be the changes that occur in other lives . . . through you.

In summary, here are key precautions to take with regard to spiritual service:

Check the attitude quotient.

Check the balance factor.

Check the power source.

These are your *rules for the road!*

Notes

1. Jack Taylor, *The Key to Triumphant Living* (Nashville: Broadman Press, 1971), p. 83.

2. Ian Thomas, *The Saving Life of Christ* (Grand Rapids: Zondervan Publishing House, 1968), p. 65.

3. Sam Shoemaker, *Extraordinary Living for Ordinary Men* (Grand Rapids: Zondervan, 1965), p. 125.

13
For Church Use Only

I recall how surprised I was, in my first years as a young pastor, to find it was the oft-recurring *small* problems, not the few *big* ones that bottomed me out! It is amazing how many little things can frustrate a young pastor with the weight of a lost world on his shoulders. A habit which really irritated me was the tendency of our people to borrow an object from the church building, then forget to return it. Over a brief period it seemed that every-other-time we needed a typewriter, adding machine, film projector, punch bowl, lawn mower, coffee maker, or our 'extra' set of folding chairs . . . a church member had them out.

One day I put a stop to it. Reasoning that these were tools to be used for God's work, I went throughout the church building and placed labels on everything not bolted down (including all the hymnals). The label read, "For Church Use Only." Needless to say, this caused some discussion!

We take numerous other things out of the church . . . *intangible* things. The most notable of which is our spiritual ministry.

There are a lot of folks today who do not mind "helping God out" a little, as long as they do not have to do it through the church. Indeed, it is amazing how many factors mitigate against any responsible, united effort for God. So many *older adults* no longer want to get that involved. Our *middle age* "Jet Set" chafe at the "drag" of cooperative effort. Our *young couples* have just broken away from the shackles of home and don't want to be accountable to others. And our *college and career-age singles* are far too "peer-group" conscious to get interested in churchwide objectives. *Society* as a whole remains so anonymous that people do not even know their neighbor's name, let alone bear common burdens. And our *old nature* (the "flesh," that inherent inner tendency to say "I want what I want when I want it") cries out to "do your own thing" . . . doing what you want, the way you want, when you want to." No! There is not much natural incentive for sacrificial, cooperative ministry among us.

Nevertheless, there is still a sense in which I believe some things are "For Church Use Only," and Christian service is one of them. We serve God *together!*

The one "umbrella" concept which encompasses all the Bible has to say about ministry is the biblical analogy of "body." "So it is with Christ's body. We are all parts of it, and it takes every one of us to make it complete, for we each have a different work to do. So we belong to each other, and each needs all the others" (Rom. 12:4-5, TLB).

Furthermore, there is a spiritual law which expresses this "body" concept of Christian service, as it is set forth in the Scriptures. "Diversity within unity" . . . that is the one fundamental rule which should govern all Christian service. While Christians serve in a variety of ways, we are always to function within a unity of effort.

So one of the most vital aspects to learn about Christian service is that it should always be executed in cooperation with the total effort of a New Testament Church . . . within a unity of effort! God always intends you to serve in harmony with others, which means you govern your efforts, even restrict them when necessary. Two are stronger than one when the two commit themselves to a common objective. And in the process of learning to serve with others, God can use their lives like laminated wood to strengthen your own and make you a greater witness of him. Biblically speaking, there is no such thing as an "independent" Christian.

The same should be said about *spiritual gifts*. They have a diversity of functions, but should be executed within a unity of effort, cooperating with the other members of the church body to accomplish unified goals. Indeed, the gifts of the spirit are for church use only: "And God hath set some in the church" (1 Cor. 12:28). "We . . . are one body . . . having . . . gifts differing" (Rom. 12:5-6). If God led you to the church you are in, he placed you there with full knowledge of the spiritual gift you have. Surely he expects you to function right there . . . unless he leads you elsewhere by *other* means of communication! But even then, the only live option for the Christian is *which* church to join. "Individual Christianity is a self-contradiction." You cannot do God's work alone. What good is a hand apart from arms, or feet apart from legs, or nose apart from head? Any one of these is useless apart from the other. That is the meaning of the "body" concept: "The eye cannot say unto the hand, I have no need of thee: nor again the head to the feet, I have no need of you" (1 Cor. 12:21). Ye are the body of Christ, and members in particular" (1 Cor. 12:27). Each member must function *in harmony* with the body!

However, we need a challenge to change! The church of our day must come around to a few things if we are to ever help our laymen fulfill God's will for their lives . . . especially in terms of lay ministry. But the church seems allergic to change. Man clings to the familiar!

No one has captured the traumatic difficulty of structural changes within the church more graphically than Ralph Neighbour, in his book *The Seven Last Words of the Church*. He suggests these words might well be: *We never tried it that way before*. Dr. Neighbour states: "Everything is in the process of change . . . in spite of this, the church continues to propagate itself, using a system and a program which have remained virtually unchanged in its basic conceptions for seventy-five years." [1] The book is the story of an experimental church, The West Memorial Baptist Church, of Houston, Texas. Now get this, the church was organized *for the very purpose of being an experimental church* "to create a divergent pattern of organization."

Nevertheless, the struggles that ensued from breaking with tradition and establishing new methods were so traumatic that the church labored months under the impending threat of a split. And the pastor at one time resigned only to return a year later and follow through with the ministry. Here you have an adventurous, aggressive, and creative people, with a pastor of Ralph Neighbour's spiritual stature . . . struggling to right the boat amidst winds of change. *Now I ask you, if they have such difficulty with change . . . what will it be like for the rest of us?* The earnest account of this great pastor should be required reading for every Christian because "*rigidity* of methods and styles will be *the* problem of tomorrow."

Nevertheless, I want to wade right in with a challenge for change. We must begin sometime, somewhere. And I believe three organizational adaptations would afford tremendous release for the exercise of lay ministry in our present-day churches.

First, *the church must come around to altering its form of worship.* The worship service must be made conducive to lay participation. If the laity are to be personally engaged in such activities as prophecy, exhortation, evangelizing, and be free to seek God for miracles and healing . . . they must be *drawn in* and *turned on!* A seminary professor, Dr. John Newport, has said that the reason for contemporary interest in glossolalia can be seen in terms of a reaction to a *nonparticipating culture* in church life.

Laymen must be "drawn in" to increased participation in our worship services. Inject dialogue. Encourage spontaneous testimony as a means of exhortation. Insert a prayer-for-healing time. Use laymen to read the Scriptures and counsel those who wish to seek God. Allow laymen to preach, sing, promote and instruct. Listen to them!

Most of all, laymen must have a time when they can "report in" to the rest of the body concerning their activities. They need to be accountable for their service-gift to the body, and they need the body's confirmation. Such a report time should be structured-in at least once every month (weekly is preferable), and the body must learn to respond to each member. For the most part, however, these should only be "news reports"; let the pastor *"editorialize."* Deacons should also be encouraged to receive such "reports" personally, dispensing instruction and encouragement. If you will allow this personal reference: our three daughters have never shared anything with me that is unimportant! Long ago I learned it was imperative that I stop to listen every time they have something to say. God's children also need an opportunity to verbalize to responsive ears.

Laymen must be drawn in, but they must also be "turned on." Too often our worship services are "locked in" to a set pattern. Each hymn, announcement period, and Scripture reading have their accustomed place in the printed program, from which we never deviate. But we must acclimate our worship services. Allow time for people to be more relaxed and expressive. Occasionally pull the anthems down lower. Sift out some ritual and sing the contemporary. Encourage congregational singing and open up for times of earnest prayer. Rearrange the order. Get high on praise. Make room for warm greetings. Be long on instruction. Hang loose in fellowship and always lead up to God . . . then out to service. The worship hour must be supercharged with spiritual electricity and wired for practical application. It must operate on the plane of the personal to enlighten your intellect, *and* challenge your will, *and* warm your heart! President James McCord of Princeton Theological Seminary was speaking of the staid, main-line denominational churches when he said: "The current Pentecostal movement may be God s judgment on the more normative churches for their coldness and formality."

Please notice that I said *allow times* for a more relaxed worship service. I did not suggest that we switch entirely. Both styles are needed. Only one becomes a "form," hence "formal!"

Secondly, *the church must come around to altering its form of workmanship.* I am not certain any of us have fully calculated the severe warp factor in the veering turn most churches must take while coming around to align their work with the Word. Just consider the changes involved in altering our form of work as it relates to the teaching about *spiritual gifts.*

It seems to me that the proper way to determine a church program is go to the Bible for *axioms* (self-evident facts) from which you can deduct some good scriptural *stratagems* (plans and procedures).

Ralph Neighbour first drew my attention to the practical ramifications of all that is said in 1 Corinthians 12.[2] From this chapter I have postulated certain *axioms* concerning the kind of program procedures most conducive to the function of spiritual gifts and I have deducted some procedural *stratagems.*

Axioms	Stratagems
Axiom #1—The church is to function as one body with many members (1 Cor. 12:12,17).	Each member of the church is a minister but should serve in unity with fellow members.
Axiom #2—The Holy Spirit provides each member with a gift	The church teaching program must fully enlighten each member

(enabling) to fulfill a particular service in and through the body for the profit of all (vv. 4,7). Each member is to major in that area as his basic ministry.

Axiom #3—The body's activity is equal to the various functions of its members, nothing more (vv. 15-17).

Axiom #4—Each member's function is vital to the body . . . and he should serve in that capacity (vv. 18-21).

Axiom #5—God leads each member to a function by which he can best *execute* his spiritual gift in and through the body (vv. 18,28).

Axiom #6—The church staff and training force are to equip each member for his function (1 Cor. 12:18,28; Eph. 4:12, a companion passage).

of the privilege and responsibility of exercising his gift.

Any church function that cannot be maintained without constant pastoral pressure upon the people, should be allowed to die a natural death (Robert Girard).

A member should not be fulfilling a major function for which he is not gifted.

The church nominating committee must recognize a member's gift and function, then fit the program to him . . . rather than determine the program, then seek individuals to staff it.

The true effectiveness of a church, in terms of service, will equal the ability of its training force to help each member develop and execute his spiritual gift . . . and fulfill his redemptive mission in this world.

The scope of this book will not allow for elaboration on these axioms and stratagems. However, they strike at the very heart of the need for churches to change their form of work (operational procedures) in order for spiritual gifts to become a practical reality.

To begin with you might review the stratagem which corresponds to axiom #5: "The church nominating committee must recognize a member's gift and function, then fit the program to him." To the contrary, most churches carry out their work by determining certain projects to be accomplished. Then they seek to enlist the personnel to get it done. But this procedure should be reversed. If spiritual gifts are selected by God (and they are), and if spiritual gifts refer to the basic function of a church member in service (and they do), then it is most reasonable to conclude that a church should determine the spiritual gifts of its work force first, and then determine its goals and programs. David Haney points out that the first method is *program-centered*, the second is *people-centered*. He refers to the program-centered approach as the "Cinderella syndrome"—one size shoe has to fit everyone.[3]

Why not take spiritual gifts seriously? Instead of conjuring up a program, then fitting people into it; seek rather to discover people's gifts and ministries, then fit the program to them. Place the priority on the pew!

Thirdly, *the church must come around to altering its form of fellowship*. Somehow our churches must accept the spiritual responsibility for maintaining opportunities of fellowship which are conducive to the discovery, development, and deployment of lay ministry. It is fundamental that we realize this will necessitate some form of *small-group* relationships . . . which present-day Sunday School classes are failing to provide. Larry Richards has suggested the development of what he calls *growth cells* of small size where intimate fellowship can support and stimulate the weakest member, and meaningful interchange takes place between fellow-members:

> Maximum spiritual growth . . . takes place in close fellowship with other believers. Yet in today's church most of our meetings are impersonal. We come to church only to sit and listen. Any conversation with others is usually on a superficial level—"Yes it is not." "Did you hear about Brother Brown?" Even in prayer meetings we do not share.[4]

As much as we need an opportunity to gather with the full body of believers, the church must also provide structures through which the members can form intimate relationships with each other, where they can hurt together and rejoice together and encourage one another. And where each member is encouraged to find that *particular mission* to which God is calling him for the week ahead.

Robert Girard has recorded the steps his church took in their search for some way to function as the body of Christ. He reports:

> We chose small groups as our chief *modus operandi*. They seemed to

us to be the nearest thing we had seen to be the kind of natural setting where the life of the church could become 'The *Shared* Life.' They seemed the kind of church structure which would allow the Holy Spirit the most freedom to do what he wanted to do in and through the Body.[5]

I am of the personal persuasion that our present-day *small-group* phenomena (as mentioned in chapter 1) is but the natural result of real spiritual renewal which has drawn hungry people together for more bread and battered servants together for mutual, personal encouragement. We *need* one another. It is a matter of spiritual survival. Perhaps many churches *are* able to provide such intimate personal fellowship through existing structures, like Bible classes. But voices are abroad which opt for the establishment of special small group cells . . . for growth, encouragement, help in decision making, prayer, and all those necessary ingredients of fellowship which give us courage for the conflict of ministering in an alien world. For example, Larson and Osborne have said: "The life of the congregation in the emerging Church will probably be structured around small groups of believers." [6] Indeed, they admit that small groups do not automatically bring vitality, *and admit that a group can be sick, deadly, oppressive, sterile, or unreal.* But they go so far as to say: "Nevertheless, we do not know of a single church now producing live laymen that does not have at its heart some form of small group fellowship." [7]

For one thing, all of us need an intimate relationship with a group of significant others in our church so they can affirm our spiritual gift. They will have witnessed the work of God through our lives and can best confirm God's use of us.

Is this not precisely what is meant by the New Testament practice of "ordination"? The word *ordination* itself refers to being "set aside" for a specific task. When I was ordained as a "minister of the gospel," my understanding of that experience was that the people of my home church, who knew my life best, *were but confirming God's gift in me.* They gave earthly confirmation to a heavenly ordination, that God had set me apart for the task of proclaiming his message to men.

There is also a sense in which your fellow Christians should *ordain* you to the effort for which you are "gifted." Of course, this is not to suggest that you be ordained in the way we ordain the pastor of a church. But others can provide you with a human affirmation of the area in which you are gifted.

Your fellow Christians can evaluate your gift by its fruit. But what is fruit? *Your fruits are those things which others can pick off of you and take with them, for themselves.* For example, the fruit is not a blessing to the tree itself, but to others. So, your gift will be evidenced by what happens in the lives of others.

It is a consistent biblical principle that a tree can be known by its fruit, "By their fruits ye shall know them" (Matt. 7:20). Some people are so knowledgable and discerning that they can identify a fruit tree by its *foliage*. That is, they can look at your natural temperament and talent, then almost tell you the area in which you will be gifted. For example, you might expect a sensitive, compassionate, selfless person to have the gift of showing mercy. However, while it takes discernment to identify a tree by its foliage, most anyone can identify your gift by its fruit. Oranges indicate an orange tree. Apples indicate an apple tree. Just so:

> Consistently fruitful *messages* indicate a gift in the area of *prophecy*,
> Consistently fruitful *service* indicates a gift in the area of *ministry*,
> Consistently fruitful *instruction* indicates a gift in the area of *teaching*,
> Consistently fruitful *counsel* indicates a gift in the area of *exhortation*,
> Consistently fruitful *self-sacrifice* indicates a gift in the area of *giving*,
> Consistently fruitful *leadership* indicates a gift in the area of *ruling*,
> Consistently fruitful *benevolence* indicates a gift in the area of *showing mercy*.

Be desperately honest with yourself at this point. Ask yourself two questions: (1) Did God empower your gift; (2) Have others recognized your gift? If the answer to either of these questions is no, this is God's "TILT" sign. You must keep in mind that possibly there is something within your life which grieves or quenches the Holy Spirit's power, thus limiting the effects of your gift! However, the Christian who is dedicated enough to seek his gift will likely be spiritual enough to be used of God to some effect! If the effects are not forthcoming, you must check the spiritual condition of your life, but it is more likely you have misunderstood the nature of your gift. Seek counsel or seek God anew to determine if your enablement is not within some other area.

One way or another the church must establish a congregational life-style which is lived out so intimately that I can help you fulfill your ministry, and you can help me fulfill mine. Of this one thing I am sure: I can best find and follow God's will in terms of service while in company with a spiritual fellowship of significant others.

Surround me with fellow-laborers who wish to count for God more than they want all else. Let them draw me into an intimate fellowship of mutual concern. Let them care deeply for me, care enough to encourage me about my potential. Have them take that first step into the vulnerable position of openness, and share about their difficulties in discovering God's will, so that I will have courage enough to be honest about my own problems. Let these same comrades be spiritual enough to assure me that I can really trust God, that he *has* given me a spiritual gift, just as he promised in the Scriptures. At the same time let their love for me be mature enough to firmly hold me responsible for the discovery and development of my spiritual mission. I need them to hold me accountable!

Furthermore, let their love for me be mature enough to take the enormous risk of releasing me to do what I believe to be God's will for my life. And let our love relationship support me with such acceptance that I can risk looking foolish in my attempts to serve God. And let us be faithful to meet and help each other with growth disciplines and personal assignments for particular tasks.

In short, the church must provide a fellowship of earnest believers who will *affirm* my ministry. This will go a long way in helping me to come up with enough faith to risk doing what God calls me to do!

Why not establish a Sunday evening training session? Enlist a group of fellow "seekers" in a quest to discover God's will for your lives, especially in terms of service and spiritual gifts. (This is exactly what I would do as a pastor!) The format of this book is designed for group study. There are thirteen chapters, one for each week of a quarter.

(Thirteen weeks is a quarter of study in the church year.) In the *thirteenth* weekly meeting you should ask the church nominating committee or church staff to meet with you and share with them the kind of programs and projects needed to facilitate the expression of your gifts and ministry. But a similar study could be made on a church retreat or in a small home Bible-study groups.

However, though the *format* of the book is for groups, the *tone* of the book is personal. I have written directly to you. It is not mandatory to have others study *with* you, for a world awaits a ministry *from* you, fellowship will result as you serve, and the way to learn is by doing. Go it alone, if necessary, but find God's will for your life—and follow it!

Notes

1. Ralph Neighbour, *"The Seven Last Words of the Church"* (Grand Rapids: Zondervan, 1973), p. 30.

2. Ralph W. Neighbour, Jr., *"This Gift is Mine"* (Nashville: Broadman Press, 1974), p. 30.

3. Haney, p. 70.

4. From the article *"Twentieth Century Re-formation,"* published in *Evangelical Action Magazine,* Wheaton, Illinois.

5. Robert O. Girard, *Brethren Hang Loose* (Grand Rapids: Zondervan, 1972), p. 131.

6. Larson and Osborne, p. 59.

7. Larson and Osborne, p. 94.

GUIDESHEET

Take this guidesheet with you in your prayertime and ask yourself these questions in the Lord's presence.

I. **For Momentary Decisions: Look Within** (What is your inner leading?)
Ask yourself two questions:

1. Are you in a position to discern God's self-less perspective?
Are you maintaining a life-style of daily self-denial, in sacrificial service to others?

> If not I would frankly advise you to temporarily consult a **Spiritual Parent** for much of your guidance . . . as Paul was the spiritual parent of Timothy (1 Tim. 1:2).

2. Are you really willing to do God's will, whatever it is?
Is Christ the Lord (boss) of your life? Does he "call the shots"? Are you really attempting to do all you know to do of God's will right now?

> This has reference to praying each day like we mentioned at the close of chapter eight, and following through in obedience.

If so . . . prayerfully choose against your own self-will, claim the mind of Christ by faith, and determine what your deepest "inner leading" is

My "inner leading" is:

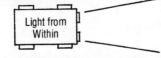

Light from Within

_____ _____

_____ _____

Don't forget your fog lights . . . if no inner leading, **fast and pray** for one!

II. **For Major Decisions: The Second Look** (when time allows—test your "inner leading".)

God will never lead you "contrary" to:	Contradictions:	Final Thoughts:
1. **Your Road Map — Scriptures** Is your inner leading contrary to the teaching, or principles, or the very sense of scripture?	"Be not slothful in business (Rom. 12:11) . . . can we financially afford to take this meeting?	"He who shuts his ears to the cry of the poor will be ignored in his own time of need" (Prov. 21:13, TLB) They need our help!
2. **Your Red Lights — God's Character** (1) Is your inner leading contrary to God's **ways:**		

God will never lead you "contrary" to:	Contradictions:	Final Thoughts:
God's **Truthfulness:** is your inner leading deceptive? Is it based upon a lie?	Has the Pastor been "talked in" to having us, or has God really led this?	Further, telephone conversation has assured me this is not the case.
God's **Love** — Is your inner leading selfish? Is it motivated by greed or lust? Is it unsympathetic or inconsiderate of others? Is it the easy way out of a situation?		
God's **Spirituality** — Is your inner leading motivated by an over-concern for material things, rather than your spiritual well-being?		
God's **Humility** — Is your inner leading influenced by envy or vanity?		
God's **Omniscience** — Is your inner leading vague or indistinct?	Indistinct leading as of now.	Getting more distinct!
God's **Omnipotence** — Is your inner leading meager, faithless, and unworthy of an all-powerful God?		
God's **Omnipresence** — Is your inner leading ultra-humanistic, has it failed to reckon with the difference God can make in the situation?		
God's **Graciousness** — Is your inner leading hard-headed and unyielding?		
God's **Infinity** — Is your inner leading flippant, frivolous, or trite?		

God will never lead you "contrary" to:	Contradictions:	Final Thoughts:
God's **Wrath** — Is your inner leading irresponsible or unlicensed?		
God's **Justice** — Is your inner leading inconsiderate or impulsive and irrational?		
(2) Is your inner leading contrary to Godly **wisdom:** Godly wisdom is **pure** — do you vacillate between decisions? Are you wavering in your conclusions?		
Godly wisdom is **peaceable** — Is your intended course of action devisive? Will it cause strife?		
Godly wisdom is **easy to be entreated** — among the spiritual, are you the only one who thinks your way? Does it make you nervous or irritable when people question your reasoning? Are you unapproachable?		
Godly wisdom is **full of mercy and good fruits** — Is your decision one of pure self-interest? Will its consequence (fruits) be harmful?		
Godly wisdom is **impartial** — Have you been influenced by prejudice or preconceived ideas? Is your inner leading narrow-minded, unfair, or too provincial?	Is my love for this friend causing me to want to go?	While praying today I definitely felt a tug of the Spirit to go!

God will never lead you "contrary" to:	Contradictions:	Final Thoughts:
Godly wisdom is **without hypocrisy** — Are you defensive? Are you slow to distrust yourself? Do you have an ulterior motive?		
3. **Your Stop Signs — Circumstances** Has God failed to confirm your inner leading with some bit of news, some inexplicable happening, some unique incident, or some additional factor that will verify your thinking?	The week they want me to come would require driving it in two days, both ways, that will be physically taxing . . . is this a negative circumstance?	A date change has relieved the time factor one way . . . and I believe a Merciful God would have me go regardless how tiring!
4. **Your Compass — Conscience** Have you failed to ask, "what you **ought** to do"? Do you lack a deep peace of mind about your inner leading? Do you have a troubled conscience about your intended course of action?		**Found Peace,** . . . will go!

Don't forget your **fog lights** — If you consistently fail to get a confirmation, put out a **fleece!**